MORE
THAN A
UNIFORM

MORE
THAN A
UNIFORM

A Navy Woman
in a
Navy Man's World

Captain Winifred Quick Collins

with Herbert M. Levine

University of North Texas Press
Denton Texas

5   4   3   2   1

The paper in this book meets the minimum requirements of the American National Standard for Permanence of Paper for Printed Library Materials, Z39.48-1984.

Permissions
University of North Texas Press
PO Box 13856
Denton TX 76203

Library of Congress Cataloging-in-Publication Data

Collins, Winifred Quick, 1911-
    More than a uniform : a Navy woman in a Navy man's world / by Winifred Quick Collins, with Herbert M. Levine ; foreword by Arleigh Burke.
        p.   cm.
    Includes index.
    ISBN 1-57441-022-9 (paper : alk. paper)
    1. Collins, Winifred Quick, 1911-   . 2. United States. Navy—Officers—Biography. 3. United States. Navy—Women.   I. Levine, Herbert M.   II. title.
V63.C65A3   1997
359'.0082'0973—dc21   96-29497
                                                       CIP

Cover design by Layton Graphics
Interior design by Accent Design and Communications
All photographs not otherwise marked are
courtesy of Captain Winifred Collins

For my beloved husband, Rear Admiral Howard Lyman Collins, USN, and to America's finest World War II WAVES who are "still something special" and to the wonderful navy women who followed them.

CONTENTS

In appreciation to the many friends who have encouraged and helped me, I wish to thank Admiral and Mrs. Arleigh Burke, Admiral and Mrs. George Anderson, Vice Admiral and Mrs. William Lawrence, Vice Admiral and Mrs. Joe Metcalf, Mr. Carl Wenz, Rear Admiral Fran McKee, USN (Rtd), and Captain Winifred Love, USN (Rtd). I am indebted to Regina Akers, Archivist, Naval Historical Center, and to Professor Linda Grant DePauw of George Washington University for their valuable assistance and encouragement. And I am also grateful to the members of the University of North Texas Press for their great help, particularly Frances Vick and Charlotte Wright.

FOREWORD

I n one sense, *More Than a Uniform* is the story of Captain Winifred Quick Collins, an extraordinary navy personality who progressed from pioneer to the leader of other pioneers. In another sense, however, it is more than that. Her individual story is synonymous with the coming of age of women in the United States Navy. It is also the story of dedicated and patriotic women who believed in themselves and in what they could contribute to the navy and to their country.

Ensign Quick was a member of the first group of 119 women who responded to their country's call in the early days of World War II. She was commissioned as an ensign in the WAVES (Women Accepted for Volunteer Emergency Service) on 4 August 1942. The initial mission of the WAVES was to release a man to fight at sea. As the war progressed, it became expedient to use more women to staff navy stations ashore. By the time of Japan's surrender, 86,000 WAVES were serving their country in 900 naval activities.

Those wartime years were times of challenge and opportunity for young WAVES, and Ensign Quick made the most of both. Her leadership ability was recognized early. In 1944, Lieutenant Quick was ordered to Pearl Harbor to determine assignments for the 5,000 women officers and enlisted who were to be sent there in the next few months. Shortly after she arrived in Pearl Harbor, Fleet Admiral Chester Nimitz invited her to a luncheon with his operational staff, a most impressive event for Lieutenant Quick, the first WAVE lieutenant assigned to Pearl Harbor.

In 1948, a law was passed authorizing women to become a part of the reserve and regular military forces. Lieutenant Commander Quick was one of the first group of women officers commissioned in the U. S. Navy Reserve. At that time, although women were achieving great success, their numbers were restricted by law as were their opportunities for promotion and higher rank. Women officers also had to retire at an earlier age than their male counterparts. Until the 1960s, there was no National Organization for Women beating the drum for equal rights. At the time Captain Quick was contributing to the advancement of women in the navy, the enormous societal changes which have supported women in the workplace were still in the future. In a tradition-bound service, equality for women was the antithesis of the warrior. The "Navy Blue Jacket" was not a *woman*. The women of Captain Collins's generation not only had to institute a tradition of competence, but they had to create their own sense of "belonging," traditions which benefit today's women in command at sea and ashore, and in senior flag positions.

Perhaps the most important characteristic of the revolution begun by Captain Collins and the other women pioneers in the service of the navy is that they fought their battles within the system. They did not tack to the mast a challenge to male leadership. There were no lists of demands or public confrontations. These women accomplished their goals with patience, intelligence, and a total loyalty and dedication to the navy. Winnie and the women of her generation were unstoppable because they believed that what they wanted was best for the navy.

On the other hand, the majority of males, both inside and outside the navy, considered it an article of faith that women could not meet the demands of the profession. Male opposition was not founded on the *fear* that women would displace men; it was *sine qua non* that they could not. Slowly prevailing, women proved their worth through performance. They showed how the navy needed them at the time and how it would continue to need them in the future.

I was chief of naval operations in 1957 when Commander Quick was selected as our top woman leader and promoted to captain. I had never met her but I had carefully reviewed her record of fifteen years of naval service. She had an outstanding record of diverse and responsible assignments. In every fitness report, from ensign to her present rank, her commanding officer had praised her leadership qualities.

Captain Winifred Quick Collins was the right person at the right time and was perfectly suited by temperament and experience to be a leader of navy women. She had the senior male officers and the civilian leaders of the navy behind her. She led, neutralized, and charmed, but always stood her ground in what she proposed for navy women. In the five years she led the women of the navy, their numbers increased, as did educational and assignment opportunities. This is not to say that there were no rocks or shoals during these years, but by the end of 1962 she had plotted the course allowing women to become an increasingly important part of the navy. Only the law restricted them.

I think, as does my wife Bobbie, that Captain Winifred Quick Collins is one of the finest persons we have ever known. We hold her in high esteem and appreciate all that she has done for this wonderful navy of ours. Today's women who are ship commanders and astronauts, who wear wings and the badges of surface warfare officers on combat ships, are in her debt. So is the entire navy of today and tomorrow.

As we say in the navy, "Well done Captain Collins. Signalman 'Two Block Bravo Zulu.'"

Arleigh Burke
Admiral, U.S. Navy (Retired)
Former Chief of Naval Operations, U.S. Navy

PREFACE

On July 30, 1942, President Franklin D. Roosevelt signed Public Law 689, granting authority for the U.S. Navy to accept women into the naval reserve in both commissioned and enlisted status. A few days later, I was one of the first women to be commissioned as an officer in the naval reserve. Since navy women were volunteers rather than draftees, we became known as Women Accepted for Volunteer Emergency Service (WAVES).

When I joined the WAVES, the idea of women serving in the military establishment was still controversial. Although women had enrolled in the navy as nurses in 1908, they were a separate corps of the navy and were not commissioned officers. Women served as yeomen in World War I but they were discharged by December 1919. In 1941, Congress established the Women's Auxiliary Army Corps (WAAC). Although this development allowed women to serve in a military status, the WAACs were not a part of either the regular army or the reserve army, holding auxiliary status instead. The navy became the first service to *commission* women—a breakthrough in the history of U.S. military personnel. I was as proud to serve the navy when I entered in 1942 as an ensign, the lowest officer rank, as I was when I retired in 1962, at what was then the highest rank—captain—which only one navy woman line officer could hold.

In this period of twenty years (1942–1962), I witnessed the transformation of the status of women in the navy. The demands of World War II produced impressive changes. In 1942, the navy planned for a maximum of 11,000 women, including officers and enlisted. By the end of the war in 1945, it had 86,000 women in its service. The role of navy women in World War II started out as mere replacements who would "release a man to fight at sea." During the course of the war, however, women very successfully took on a wide variety of nontraditional jobs, consequently becoming an essential part of the navy's war effort. Not all navy women were sent home after World War II because many were needed to assist in the demobilization process. Then in 1948, in order to have a trained cadre of veteran navy women ready for the anticipated large influx of women recruits in the event of another major war, Congress passed legislation permitting a small number of women to stay on active duty and become part of the regular navy.

From 1948 to 1962, one objective of these veteran leaders was to expand the kinds of assignments for both women officers and enlisted women, with the result that navy women were gradually accepted for positions of increased responsibility. These leaders began to work toward improving recruiting, expanding job assignments, and enhancing training and education. But they were not engaged in a mere holding pattern; instead they were aggressively charting new roles and taking on assignments in new technical areas such as jet aviation and nuclear-powered ships.

When I think about the twenty years of my service, I am astonished by the profound changes that navy women experienced. As reservists, navy women could not be called up involuntarily during World War II. They were placed in positions where they could not normally give orders to men who held lower rank. Until mid-1942, they could only train at all-female schools. Until 1943, when an amendment to the law establishing the WAVES raised the highest rank for a woman to captain (and then to only one woman at a time), the highest rank a woman could hold was lieutenant commander. Until 1944, when they were permitted to serve in the Hawaiian Islands, they were restricted to assignment in the continental United States. Also in that year, women were selected to be flight orderlies with the Naval Air Transport Service.[1] But they could not be in combat, or fly planes, or—with the exception of nurses—serve on navy ships or planes.

By the time I left in 1962, all of these limitations had ended, with the exception of combat restrictions. Women were part of the regular navy. Female naval reservists could be called up involuntarily just like male naval reservists—a practice that began for women during the Korean War (1950–1953). Women officers could give orders to men of lower rank. They could serve not only in the continental United States but in installations and shore establishments throughout the world. They could train at specialized schools and graduate schools with their male counterparts. They could fly noncombat navy planes and serve on noncombat ships. Female naval officers could train in personnel management, foreign languages, intelligence, comptrollership, management, cryptology, business administration, meteorology, communications engineering, merchandising, disbursement, financial management, logistic planning, public relations, educational training, mathematics, political science, and air-ocean environment. Enlisted navy women could be assigned to duty as aerographers, air controlmen, storekeepers, photographers, yeomen, radiomen, communications technicians, personnel specialists, machine accountants, disbursing clerks, journalists, hospital and dental technicians, draftsmen, opticalmen, lithographers, instrumentsmen, data technicians, X-ray technicians, and link trainers[2]—even if the official titles of their jobs did not reflect the fact that a woman was performing the work. By the time I left the navy, navy women received the respect which came with a rank. Moreover, they had authority that surpassed that granted to many other professional women in American society, to the extent that when they held a particular rank, they got the exact same pay as their male counterparts.

Although they were impressive, the gains women made during the twenty years of my service career should not be overstated. The number of female officers and enlisted women serving in occupations considered nontraditional in civilian society in 1962 cannot compare to the number of navy women who were still working in traditional occupations such as administration, personnel, supply, and health care. Complete gender equality was not a reality. Some navy men still refused to grant navy women the respect their rank deserved. And even though their pay rate was the same as that of men of equal rank, women did not receive the same allowances and incentive pay (e.g., married housing allowances) as did males who were married. This situation did not change until 1973 when a Supreme Court decision gave military women's spouses equal privileges with military men's spouses. That same year, pregnancy was declared to be no longer a cause for discharge.

From the beginning of my military service until the day I left, I found that women demonstrated by their professionalism and commitment that the navy needed them if it hoped to pursue its mission successfully. Navy women have continued to show this dedication in the more than three decades since I retired.

As one of the first navy women, I was able to make my own contribution to the transformation of the navy. I was not only a witness to important events but—because of the accidents of history and personal circumstances beyond my control—I was also a participant in shaping that transformation.

My most important work began in 1957 when I was appointed assistant chief of naval personnel for women. At that time, the navy had 295 regular women line officers and 430 reserve officers on active duty, plus 100 staff regular officers and 96 reservists on active duty.[3] Enlisted strength was 4,837. At that time, the law for promotion of women line officers was based on—and restricted to—the active line strength. In contrast, the law for promotion of men line officers was based on both the regular and reserve strength of line officers. This inequity resulted in a much higher promotion percentage for male officers than for female officers. Because of this restriction, only four women officers could be promoted to the rank of commander, and four to lieutenant commander. During the ensuing five years, I made every possible effort to increase the number of regular line officers on active duty by improving the promotional opportunities for highly motivated women officers to be selected for the ranks of commander and lieutenant commander, the top ranks permitted by law with the exception of one captain of temporary rank.

When I retired in 1962, I was proud of the gains I had achieved in active strength: 345 line officers on active duty plus 61 line officers in the Indoctrination School (for a total of 406 line officers on active duty). In addition, there were 129 active duty reservists, 1,590 regular active staff officers, and 1,196 staff reservists. Enlisted strength was at 5,847. A total of 3,500 inactive officers and enlisted were in the reserves and available for recall to active duty.

The gains of navy women have not received the attention they deserve. To a great extent, the military has served as a force for social mobility for both women and minorities—to the betterment of social justice in America. Although the "woman's revolution" is often said to have begun in the early 1960s, we should recognize that at that time women in the navy were *already* performing important jobs which were unavailable to their civilian counterparts. The changes for women in the navy had become profound before the women's revolution got under way.

These changes did not come about easily. Many elected political leaders as well as many navy men shared sexist attitudes toward the role of women in society and therefore imposed obstacles to the advancement of navy women. Some men could not see women as professionals worthy of equal status. These ideas were driven by the culture of the time and were motivated by the fear that if women succeeded, they might threaten opportunities and promotions for men—"the *real* wage earners." In the twenty years of my navy service, however, I met many men who were supportive. It is clear to me—as I suspect it is to nearly all women who were my contemporaries in the navy—that the men who understood women's potential for contributing to the betterment of the navy and to our national security were indispensable in helping to effect beneficial changes in navy policy.

During my twenty-year navy life, I had some extraordinary experiences. I met some of the most outstanding military leaders of the times—Admirals Bill Halsey, Chester Nimitz, Tom Moorer, U. S. G. Sharp, Charles Duncan, Fred Boone, and George Anderson, for example. Admiral Arleigh Burke, chief of naval operations and the senior naval officer, was one of my many bosses in 1957 when I was appointed captain. I worked with gifted military and civilian people—both men and women—at all levels of professional accomplishment. It was a great personal adventure for me, and I recount the high points of that experience in this book.

I also carry my story forward to the present. I left the service thirty-five years ago and, unlike the proverbial old soldier, I did not "fade away." Instead, I have been able to participate in corporate decisions in industry as well as in top level jobs in the Navy League and other organizations. In 1972, during the Vietnam War, I accepted an assignment from Admiral E. R. Zumwalt, chief of

Admiral Arleigh Burke, chief of naval operations when Captain Collins reported from London to assume the senior job as chief of naval personnel for women. He and his wife were close friends of Captain Collins and her husband, Rear Admiral Collins. The photograph is signed "To my good friend, Captain Winifred Quick, with high esteem and in appreciation for all that she has done and is doing as Director of our splendid WAVES and for this wonderful Navy of ours." Official U.S. Navy photograph.

Admiral George Anderson, chief of naval operations, 1961-1963. Captain Collins first met him in 1944 and became close friends with him and his wife. During the time Admiral Anderson held the top job in the navy, Captain Collins was the top woman line officer. The photograph is signed "To Captain Winnie Quick Collins—Old friend, charming lady and a very distinguished naval officer who has contributed so much to making our navy 'the best that ever was.'" Official U.S. Navy photograph.

Admiral J. M. (Mike) Boorda, chief of naval operations 1994–1996. The photograph is signed "To Winnie, an outstanding naval leader whose pioneering service in the Navy has encouraged today's Navy women to build upon your successful career to become 'all that they can be.' God bless, you are a wonderful friend." Official U.S. Navy photograph.

(left) Admiral Bill Halsey, commander of Third Fleet, Pacific during the time Captain Collins served in Hawaii. He made headlines early in WWII by promising to ride a white horse in Tokyo upon the defeat of Japan. Official U.S. Navy photograph.

Vice Admiral Charles Lockwood, commander of the submarine forces in the Pacific, 1944–1946. Captain Collins met him her second day in Pearl Harbor and they became close friends. Official U.S. Navy photograph.

naval operations, that took me to South Vietnam. Whatever else I was doing, my thoughts have continued to focus on the navy and the progress of navy women.

By no means do I wish to give the impression that in 1962 women had achieved all that they needed to accomplish in the navy. I am aware that many changes have taken place since my departure, and am pleased that women have made great strides in removing such barriers to their achievement as restrictive promotion and retirement policies. It was not until 1976 that one woman—Fran McKee—became the first woman unrestricted line officer to be promoted to rear admiral. (Prior to that, Captain Alene Duerk, head of the nurse corps, was spot promoted to become an admiral as a result of legislation governing the Nurse Corps.) Women did not go before regular admirals' selection boards and were not promoted to admiral on the same basis as men until after the passage of the Defense Officer Personnel Management Act (DOPMA) in 1980. It was not until 1993 that the issue of women in combat was resolved in many areas of navy activity.

The problem of discrimination, harassment, and even violence against navy women persists although the navy has issued directives to deal with these violations. For this reason, I conclude the book with observations about the changes that have taken place for women since my departure as well as about my hopes for the future of women in the navy.

---

[1] They flew only across the United States until June 1945, at which time they were also assigned to air routes to Hawaii and Europe.

[2] Link trainers teach aviation cadets flying lessons on simulators.

[3] There are two types of line officers: unrestricted line officers and restricted line officers. Unrestricted line officers are trained and authorized to command surface ships, submarines, aircraft squadrons, shore activities and shore stations, and special duty assignments. Restricted line officers are restricted in their performance of duty and are specialists in aviation (aero-engineering, general engineering, and other specialties).

Nonline officers are called staff officers and include doctors, dentists, lawyers, nurses, medical specialists, chaplains, and construction engineers.

one

My Early Years

It would have been comforting for me to know in 1916, when I was five years old, that I would spend the most momentous chapter of my professional life in the U.S. Navy. Like most people, however, I never made a career commitment when I was young that could guide my every professional and social step along the way. For a girl in the second decade of the twentieth century, a commitment to be a naval officer would be all but impossible even to imagine because the idea of commissioning women officers was beyond anyone's serious contemplation. During my childhood—and even into my young adult years—the U.S. Navy was predominantly a male preserve—like a private gentleman's club—as it had been throughout its history.

I entered the navy in 1942 when I was thirty-one years old. Without U.S. intervention in that war, I would never have become a member of the military establishment. Quite simply, there would have been no place for women in the navy—at least at that time.

As with anyone in a new career, I carried baggage packed with experiences, training, and values which had shaped my character. My life in the years before I entered the service was by no means conventional. It was, instead, filled with widely fluctuating experiences of joy and sorrow, triumph and tragedy, and reward and set-back. No doubt, qualities of my character influenced the way I worked in the military. So it is best to begin my story with a brief description of the main features of my early years—features that had a profound impact on my military career.

⚓ ⚓ ⚓

My story begins in central Montana where I was born in 1911. My family—the Reddens—lived in Neihart, a mining town fifty miles southeast of Great Falls. At the time of my birth, I had a brother, Dan, five years older, and a sister, Evelyn, seven years older than I. My mother was named Mary Winifred; she named me Winifred Mary. Perhaps her choice of names was prophetic, for we could not have been more exact opposites. My father was Daniel A. Redden, the parent who was to have the more profound influence on my life. He was born in Middlesborough, Yorkshire, England, on March 30, 1863. When he was seventeen, his parents, staunch Roman Catholics, decided that his future lay in the church, a parental decision that he could not accept. He ran away to Canada in order to escape the priesthood. I think his flight was fortunate for the Vatican because he was certainly no conformist. He was a free spirit and an entrepreneur. I can't imagine him fitting into a clerical life.

Father went to Ontario in Canada because he had older brothers living there who were successful businessmen and also because it was open to new immigrants. Later, he traveled to Montana. I don't know for sure why he went out west, but I suspect that he was attracted by the business opportunities that the mining interests afforded. In Neihart, which was then a prosperous and booming mining town with a population of only about two thousand people, he met my mother, Mary Winifred Farrel. She was born in Rosemont, Minnesota, on October 12, 1878. Her family left their Minnesota farm for Neihart in hopes of taking advantage of the mining boom. My mother was twenty-two and my father was thirty-seven when they married.

My immediate family was very prosperous. My father and his partner owned most of the businesses in Neihart—the hotel, the restaurants, the saloons, and the mining interests. Although I was very young at the time so that my recollection is not complete, I remember that he built a special gym just for me, my brother, and my sister. He presented each Redden child with a miniature set of dumbbells and taught us to go through a series of exercises. Father believed that all his children—not just his son—should be physically strong.

He had similar ideas about the importance of education. We had a two-room library filled with wonderful, beautiful books. I don't remember who taught me to read, but I learned early. I did a lot of reading when I was young—a practice I continued through the years. In my youth, I read all kinds of books, including history and novels. I read a lot about cowboys, too. My love for books came from my father, who—although self-educated—was an avid

The Redden family c. 1913. From left to right: back row, Daniel A. (father), Evelyn (sister); front row, Winifred, Mary (mother), Dan (brother).

reader with a preference for nonfiction books, mostly history. He loved stories of the American West, particularly the pioneer days. He knew English history magnificently. Even in his nineties, he still read three or four books a week.

I recall the affluence of my earliest years in part because of the kinds of food I ate. Neihart was a rural area, remote from even the small urban center of Great Falls. But my father imported gourmet food for us. He wanted his children to have the finer things of life and also to appreciate many different kinds of food, not only because of their taste but because of their healthful properties as well. I remember learning to eat many exotic kinds of fish, and we always had oysters shipped in. My introduction to oysters was unforgettable. I couldn't have been more than three. We all sat around the dinner table, and the maid served oyster soup. My father said, "Now, Boots"—my nickname—"this is your first taste of oysters. I want you to learn to eat them, because they are very healthy for you. You're probably not going to like them, but you can't leave the table till you finish." I *didn't* like them but I ate them. I had no choice. And later I most certainly did learn to like them. I also came to love cooking and eating many other exotic foods, and I believe I have my father to thank for it. After all, he raised me to accept strange dishes.

My father brought up all of his children to be achievers, not just his son. He took an interest in our physical fitness and in our education. He used to say to me, "You're an outstanding western kid"—the kind of affectionate remark that someone could make about a boy *or* a girl. He brought me up to think that there were no insurmountable barriers to what women could accomplish. He even told me, "I hope to heaven I live long enough to see a woman president because the men have made such a mess of things." To be sure, I was aware that women did not have the opportunities that men had, but the gender disparity wasn't a problem to me.

My brother Dan was the person who christened me "Boots." I have no idea where the nickname came from except possibly the fact that I must have worn baby booties. Dan was a terrible tease, and his threats to me often became torment. He never gave up his teasing in my youth, but I always defended myself, resorting to punches when I had to. I could never understand why he persecuted me. Once, when we were both adults, I questioned him about it. He said he was sorry for making my life miserable and surmised that he might have been jealous of me. That could have been so, as I think that I was my father's favorite child. I was certainly just like my father not only in temperament and humor but also in intellectual curiosity.

When I was five, my mother somehow persuaded my father to buy her a 400-acre ranch near Missoula, in the western part of the state. It cost $20,000, which was a lot of money in 1916. The former owners had horses, cattle, and wheat, along with cowboys to work the ranch. I have no idea why my mother wanted the property. If she and my father were having problems, I was too young to know it. Maybe she wanted to prove that she was a real businesswoman, like her sister Margie Lapointe, who owned a very successful women's specialty shop. My mother, however, had no talent as a businesswoman. But I didn't care about the reasons for our move. I was thrilled at the prospect of living on a ranch and seeing real cowboys. I'm told that en route to our new home, I asked whether we were going to be "hayseeds"—hicks! Maybe I thought that in comparison to the farm, Neihart was the cradle of civilization.

I always wore dresses, as the Levi culture with its cowboy jeans hadn't yet been born—at least not in Montana and certainly not for little girls. But my life continued to include a world of material acquisitions and activities that could be considered outside the traditional female role. I had fourteen dolls, but I had my own horse, too. So obviously, I was brought up in a manner that would allow me to develop my interests and talents from a wide array of options. I recall riding horses with my neighbor's two sons, who used to try to get my horse to jump. Fortunately, I had become a fairly good rider so there were no disasters. I never once fell off a horse.

I had a free lifestyle. My mother never asked where I'd been or what I did. She was busy and assumed that I could take care of myself. I often spent the weekend at my neighbors, who enjoyed my company. The mother of my two male playmates was very kind to me, and nearly every weekend she asked my mother to let me spend the weekend with them. She always asked me to bring extra dresses, too, so she could wash and iron them for me. Perhaps I wasn't very well groomed. My mother didn't have much time for washing and ironing, as she was busy trying to run the ranch.

Still, I did not feel neglected. I could make decisions about what was good and bad for me. To my way of thinking, my family and I were having a wonderful life. Our ranch was truly in wild territory, which was home to mountain lions, bears, wolves, and coyotes. I was never afraid but once, when I was five and a half. I was out fishing alone. When I prepared to return home, I mounted my horse. Suddenly my horse started shivering. I looked behind me and saw a big black bear! I turned my horse very slowly and walked him toward the road. When we were out of sight of the bear, we took off like a firecracker and headed for home. I don't know which of us was more frightened, the horse or me.

A year after we moved to the farm, I entered the first grade in a one-room schoolhouse. In all, there were about ten students in different "grades"—from first to eighth—with one teacher to teach us all. My brother Dan and my sister Evelyn were members of that class, as were my two playmates. The teacher was a lovely Swedish woman who lived in our house on our huge ranch. I remember that she encouraged me, talked to me, and told me wonderful children's stories. I thought that when I grew up, I wanted to be a teacher just like her. Once she gave me a copy of *Peter Rabbit*. She even wrote inside the cover: "A gift to Winifred Redden for honors in spelling." The gift was a treasure to me. I still have it.

I didn't know it then but my days of affluence and a carefree existence were about to come to an end. My father's businesses in Neihart suffered economic reverses. To make matters worse, everything my mother touched was a financial disaster. My father became exasperated because he would find check after check missing from the ranch checkbook, with no record from my mother of the payee, amount, or purpose. This chaos was a reflection of both her inability to run a business and a quality of character that can best be described as trusting to the point of gullibility. People always took advantage of her kindness. For example, time after time I saw her going to the bunkhouse at nine o'clock in the morning with fresh rolls for the cowboys. Once I asked her, "Aren't cowboys supposed to be up at 5 A.M. and out with the cattle?" She did not answer.

On one visit my father told my mother that he could not continue to pour money into the ranch, as it had never made any profit and his resources were now greatly diminished. Not much later we had to sell the ranch at a great loss. The good times were now over. When I was nine years old, in third grade, we moved to Missoula, Montana, where my father bought a small hotel with the little money we had left. I remember him telling the family that we were upon hard times. My clothes were now very shabby—

a reflection of the family's dire straits. I was ashamed that I had to wear these clothes when I attended my new school—a Catholic day school.

Shortly after our move to Missoula, my brother Larry was born. From early on, I always felt a special bond with him, although I loved Dan and Evelyn, too.

By the time I reached the age of ten, I recognized that I needed to do something to bring in some money. I became an entrepreneur. I saw a newspaper advertisement for sales people to market garden seeds, and by spring I was selling the company's seeds. I also made arrangements with another company to sell its prepackaged foods which, with the addition of milk or water, became puddings or pie fillings. I had a long list of customers. I recall that some of my first profits went to buy Larry a darling sailor suit. Neither of us dreamed what a prophetic gift that would turn out to be. I delivered the products on my bike, but not everyone looked kindly on a ten-year-old girl becoming an entrepreneur. I remember that one woman said to me, "Does your mother know you're out doing this?"

"Oh, of course she does," I said. "She's already approved of it."

Maybe ten-year-old girls shouldn't lie, but I had to do something. My mother was not concerned about where I was. She was busy with her own life, and I was really my own mother. Perhaps I always had been.

Although my family's financial situation continued to deteriorate in Missoula, the hotel profits kept us solvent for a while. When I was eleven, my parents divorced—a process initiated by my mother. My father gave her the hotel and went to Oregon to seek business opportunities, but he wrote me often, and his letters were always encouraging and endearing.

I did not have the parental guidance that most children of my time and place had. I had to deal with the world as I best could manage, and I experienced early challenges in my life as a young entrepreneur. Once, the seed company I dealt with threatened me with a lawsuit. I learned that the company often used this technique to intimidate its unsuspecting salespeople into turning over part of their own profits. The company claimed that I had neither returned nor paid for the seeds I ordered. The truth was that I had most certainly paid for the seeds, and I had the money order to prove it. So I wrote back. In my childish printing, I noted: "My daughter has paid you, and I'm going to take your threat to the attorney general." I signed the letter "Mrs. Dan Redden." I never heard from the seed company again.

I continued to look for whatever jobs I could find. From early on, I did chores and odd jobs for neighbors. I babysat *and* had a paper route. Unlike Dan and Evelyn, I always had some money— although it was never very much—because I went out and made it myself. But my life as an entrepreneur was interrupted when I was eleven years old. An epidemic of infantile paralysis (polio) broke out in Missoula. Many children died, and others were disabled for life. At the time, no vaccine existed and the only treatment was rest. Polio victims were kept in isolated rooms because of the very real danger of spreading the often lethal disease.

I caught the disease, which affected my back. My sister Evelyn, at the time eighteen and engaged to be married, volunteered to nurse me, which meant that she exposed herself to the infectious disease. It was summertime, and we were totally isolated in a two-bed hospital room for three weeks. Food had to be passed through an opening in the door lest the person delivering it become a victim of polio. Evelyn's loving care helped me to recover. I was one of the lucky children who suffered no lasting physical damage from having polio, although I did undergo physical therapy for a year after leaving the hospital. I have never forgotten what Evelyn did for me or the risk she took. Later in life, I tried my best to repay her.

By the time I was recuperating at home, I realized that my mother couldn't run the hotel any better than she'd handled the ranch. We continued to lose money, and she was finally forced to sell the hotel. She went from one business disaster to another. Her next venture was a boardinghouse, which she ran in partnership with a woman I thought was disreputable. The woman was coarse, and I told my mother so. We found out later that the woman had stolen money from my gullible mother. My sister Evelyn had the same trusting nature. I think that anyone could have put anything over on either of them.

Recognizing the difficult situation I faced, my father thought it best for me to become a resident in the all-girls Catholic school I was attending. It was clear to him that my mother's boardinghouse was not a suitable place. The change was good for me, although being away from home was a difficult experience. I missed my brother Larry very much, as he was a darling child at age three. I could at least visit my family on weekends, which I did every week. But on my thirteenth birthday—which fell on a Friday in November—I experienced an unexpected surprise.

Birthdays are usually happy times for youngsters, but this was one of the unhappiest days of my life. When I arrived home from school, I found that my mother had left town, leaving no forwarding address. I was heartbroken, bewildered, and alone when I returned to school that day. Her unannounced departure was a terrible blow, and I felt miserable. I was ashamed of my mother—so ashamed that I did not tell the nuns about what she had done.

I did not hear from my mother until March, about four months after she left, when I received a strange letter from her informing me that I had won $5 in the national recipe contest I had entered before she left home. My mother informed me that she had cashed the check and kept the money. No congratulations. No explanations for her departure. At the time, moreover, that $5 would have been a fortune to me. She did mention that she was working in a bakery. Again, I was bewildered at her behavior.

She had not indicated her address on the letter, but the postmark read "Lewiston, Idaho." I knew that my Larry was with her and I missed him very much. I recognized that my mother did not want to have anything to do with me, but I wanted to see my little brother. I determined that in June—when the academic year was over—I would find them. I wrote my father and asked him for money for the train trip and he sent some, but it was only enough for a one-way ticket.

I never told him or the nuns that I didn't have my mother's address. The nuns were concerned enough about my traveling alone at age fourteen. The two-day trip required several train changes. I slept in the day coach, and during my waking hours planned how I would visit each bakery in Lewiston until I found

her. It was a big adventure for me. At the time, it never even occurred to me to worry that I would not find her.

The first thing I did when I got to town was look in the phone
book. There were only three bakeries in Lewiston. She was not at
the first two, so I was apprehensive as I headed to the third, but
my prayers were answered when I found my mother there. Unfortunately, her welcome was very chilly. She didn't even hug me,
and said simply: "How did you ever find me?" But my reunion
with four-year-old Larry was wonderful. He hadn't seen me for a
year, but he still recognized me.

My mother said that she had no room for me and no money to
support me. I had thought that there might be some little job I
could do in the bakery in exchange for my room and board, but
she took me straight to a Catholic hospital and signed me up to
work there as a cleaning aide. She knew that at the hospital, I
could get room and board in return for my work. Her unexpected
and unwanted problem of finding a "home" for me had been
solved. The job at the hospital was very depressing and lonesome.
I worked long hours with little time off. The hospital was across
town from my mother's apartment, so I never even got to visit
Larry.

During her lifetime, I never confronted my mother about why
she left Missoula and why she had no interest in me. I wanted to,
but the timing never seemed appropriate. For years, I had a great
bitterness toward her. Eventually, however, I recognized that such
an attitude was not good for me, so I told myself that perhaps she
had experienced a bad childhood too. I eased my heart by con-

vincing myself that she did not know how to behave any better, and that the emotional harm she did was not deliberate.

With my father in Oregon experiencing difficult financial times and my mother showing utter indifference to my life, I had few places to turn. I did find help thanks to Evelyn, who had married and was living in Missouri. My brother Dan was living with them also, but would soon be moving to Seattle to attend the University of Washington. Evelyn wanted to see my mother and Larry, and wrote me that in June she would be visiting Lewiston and would take me back with her to Missouri. I was thrilled at the idea.

After a week's visit with my mother, Evelyn returned to Missouri, and I was with her. The living conditions were somewhat confining. Evelyn and her husband had a small one-bedroom apartment, and I slept in the living room. Evelyn worked full-time, so I always had dinner ready when they came home, and I also did the family wash. Although the physical conditions were not ideal, I was still glad to have a place I could call home and be near my sister. I also became friends with a girl my own age who lived in the building. But even this little bit of happiness did not last. My brother-in-law began to pay a great deal of attention to me. He tried to get me to kiss and hug him, and his actions made me very nervous. I told Evelyn about it, but she said not to worry, he just "liked" me. But after he tried to get me to undress one time, I fled to my girlfriend's apartment in terror. Her mother was shocked. She told me to get my clothing when he was away, and come to live with them. After a few weeks, I realized that I couldn't sponge off my friend's family for long. My sister wanted me to come back, but I couldn't bear to.

Through the high school I was attending, I found a job which offered room, board, and a weekly pittance, working for a young couple who had one child. They were pleasant to me, but they never seemed to realize the loneliness of my life. I had no companionship whatsoever. My daily routine consisted of school, lunch, and working for them. I had no time to participate in school activities, and the couple never wondered about any needs I might have. They never said, "Isn't there something going on in high school?" "Aren't there friends you'd like to see?" They never even asked me whether I'd like to go to a movie.

I stayed with this family for two years. In June, the summer before my senior year in high school, I received a letter from my mother's sister, Aunt Margie, who lived in Klamath Falls, Oregon. She and her husband Charlie had a successful woman's specialty shop. She invited me to live with them for my last year in high school and told me that after I graduated, they would send me to business school, after which I could have a job in the store. Although I was thrilled with the idea of living with them, I intended to go to college, not business school. In those days "business school" meant secretarial or bookkeeping training. I didn't intend to be a secretary or a bookkeeper. I never confided my plans to Aunt Margie, though, since I did not want to hurt her feelings or jeopardize my chance to move in with her. She sent me the money for travel, and I arrived in July.

Even at that age, I had ambition. I knew that I wanted to go to college but I had no burning commitment to a particular profession. Like many young people, at times I thought that maybe I would be a teacher, nurse, librarian, or doctor. But most of all, my ambition was to be successful. I thought, too, that I wanted one day to get married.

My aunt gave me some pretty clothes—the nicest I ever had. She moved me to a separate apartment, and she brought her elderly father (my grandfather) to live with me. My job was to keep the apartment clean and cook meals for him.

I was happy in school. I found some very nice classmates—both girls and boys. Although I was a stranger to their group, they elected me president of one of the school clubs. I was thrilled with my new honor and with the fun we all had together. My newfound happiness was not to last, however. Two or three times a year my aunt went on buying trips to New York. She left for one such trip the October after I'd moved in with my grandfather. While she was gone, my uncle had me come down to the store to pick out some new dresses. Then he started wanting to kiss me whenever he came to visit my grandfather and me, which was usually late because he ate his dinner downtown. I tried my best to avoid him, and I could tell that he was annoyed by my attempt to keep a distance.

When my aunt came back in late November, her husband told her I had been out late every night with boys. She never questioned me about it. She only gave me bus fare and told me that I had to leave the next day for Seattle where my brother Dan was in college. I cried most of the night. I told my wonderful friends that my mother was very ill and that I had to go to Seattle to be with her. Years later, after my aunt divorced her husband because of his numerous affairs, I told her of his attentions to me and let her know that everything her husband had said about my behavior was a lie. She only said, "I'm sorry." Period. She never asked how I'd managed to live after she threw me out.

I had no choice but to go to Seattle and impose myself on Dan's hospitality. He worked all night as a hotel desk clerk and went to college in the mornings. He was struggling financially and couldn't afford to feed me. I slept in his bed at night while he worked, and found a part-time job that provided me enough money for a sparse diet.

To make matters worse, I once again had to leave school in the middle of the academic year. When I registered for high school in Seattle, I had to take some very difficult tests. Some subjects I had studied in Missouri and Oregon weren't covered at all in Seattle. Similarly, the Seattle school system had requirements for courses I'd never had. I'm not sure how I passed the tests, but I did, allowing me to resume my senior-year standing and to graduate on schedule from Seattle's Broadway High School.

After graduation, I found a full-time job as a bookkeeper with a small Seattle company and moved into an apartment of my own. I worked a year and a half to save money for college, meanwhile sending letters to many colleges asking them about scholarships. Finally, the University of Southern California (USC) in Los Angeles offered me a small scholarship sponsored by Lucien Brunswig, president of a pharmaceutical company. I gratefully accepted. When I arrived in Los Angeles, Mr. Brunswig asked to meet me. To my good fortune, he offered me a part-time job at the Brunswig

Company. The job offer was the best financial opportunity I could hope to get, and I happily grabbed it. My salary was $50 a month.

I worked twenty-five hours a week in Mr. Brunswig's banking department—balancing accounts—while carrying sixteen units a semester in college. I majored in business administration and minored in art—a combination that reflected my diverse interests. After I graduated in 1935, Mr. Brunswig said, "How would you like to work for me full-time?" In spite of the fact that he appreciated the work I was doing and wanted me to continue my employment at his company, I was disappointed. I had expected my college education to open up new opportunities. But the nation was still in the midst of the Depression, so I asked him, "What do you want me to do?"

Winifred Redden, 1933, in Los Angeles. Modeling for a millinery designer was one of the many jobs Winifred held while attending the University of Southern California.

He answered: "Find something you like, and you'll work out of the president's office." It was a fine offer. I wanted to apply the knowledge I had gained from my business courses at USC, so I told him I wanted to be the personnel director, and he agreed. Working out of Mr. Brunswig's office gave me a considerable advantage within the company, as it placed me in a position to understand the entire operations of the organization. My hope of applying what I had learned at USC was soon realized. Personnel directors are specialists who develop job descriptions, investigate the types of skills needed to perform those jobs, and establish the pay levels. They do not exclusively focus on the needs of an employer, however. They are also involved in planning employee career ladders.

I began my new job by analyzing the positions in the Brunswig's laboratories. At the time, only women worked in assembling the pharmaceuticals, although there were male supervisors. The women worked at similar tasks, but there were wide disparities in their wages. The reason for the pay disparities was completely idiosyncratic. That is to say, the pay for each worker depended on Mr. Brunswig's capricious decisions about individual employees. I saw that some women received higher pay because they were sycophants; others because they were charming.

Mr. Brunswig was a decent and honorable human being, and his capriciousness had no element of harassment. From a business point of view, however, his pay policy lacked an underlying rational basis—if job performance is the standard for rewarding employees. The work the women performed consisted of rather mundane tasks, such as cleaning bottles, filling the bottles and jars with drugs and cosmetics, and putting bottle covers on—work that could be easily classified and analyzed so that an employee's performance could be objectively evaluated. Two matters struck me at the beginning. First, the women were not working as efficiently as they could. And second, the idiosyncratic character of allocating pay was not only inherently unfair but was undermining staff morale as well. I asked Ada Holmes, one of my former USC professors, to help me conduct a job analysis of these employees of the company.

My report recommended wage changes to correct inequities by giving equal pay for similar tasks to laboratory employees. I also urged that an incentive system based on productivity be adopted to encourage better performance. I knew that the arguments about being fair or improving morale wouldn't work with Mr. Brunswig because in business matters he was always reluctant to spend one penny more than was absolutely necessary to get the work done. So, my major argument to him was that the pay disparities reduced productivity and subsequently lowered profits. That contention won him over.

When I asked him to announce the new pay scheme to the employees, however, he was reluctant to do so. He preferred to keep his distance from his employees, as he was a somewhat reserved person. When he asked me to make the announcement, I told him that for the changes to have any meaning to the women, he—and he alone—had to announce them. After persistent appeals on my part, he reluctantly agreed. When he gave his speech, the women immediately understood how they could realize an increase in income from the new policy. They hugged and kissed

Mr. Brunswig in appreciation. Not anticipating such an emotional demonstration of approval, he was elated. "They liked the new policy," he said to me in surprise. And he recognized that because he had made the announcement, the employees attributed the policy change to him. Fortunately for me (as well as for the company), the emotional outburst was followed by demonstrated improvement in worker performance. Productivity skyrocketed, and company profits increased. Mr. Brunswig thought he was a hero. I thought he was a hero, too.

My studies at USC and my work with Professor Holmes on the analysis of the Brunswig Company were probably responsible for the next major turning point in my life, which came after working full-time for Brunswig. My professors recommended me for a new management training program at Harvard/Radcliffe, which was the brainchild of Ada Comstock, Radcliffe's president, a remarkable person who had started many innovative academic programs for women. I was one of only five women to be admitted in the first year of that program—which was regarded at the time as only an experiment.

Although I had a good job, I did not have enough money for a year's study at Harvard. At this point I learned that although Mr. Brunswick counted every nickel from his business, he could also be very generous. He asked me how much money I would need at Radcliffe, and although I had no idea, I answered off the top of my head: "Four thousand dollars." Without blinking an eye, he said, "I'll write you a check for that much. If you need more, I'll send it. Just let me know." There were no strings attached to his offer. I didn't even have to come back to work for him afterward. I will always be grateful to Mr. Brunswig for his faith in me and his generosity. We corresponded the entire year I was at Radcliffe, and I often wrote him to tell him how appreciative I was about what he had done for me.

My decision to go off to Radcliffe was based on both professional and personal reasons. I saw it as important to my education and career, but also as a way to break away from an unhappy relationship. As typical of most young women at the time, I married right after completing college. I took the last name of my husband, Roy T. Quick. The marriage was not a success, and both my husband and I knew it. We both recognized that my year at Radcliffe would be a transition for us and would probably conclude with a divorce, which it did. I thought that I would never marry again, because I did not want to have a second failed marriage.

My experience at Harvard/Radcliffe was everything I had hoped for. We had some of the finest professors. We learned a great deal about productivity, job satisfaction, and the factors influencing employees to work harder. I enjoyed the companionship of my fellow students. President Comstock kept very close contact with me and my four classmates, sometimes even coming to our seminars. Because Harvard Business School was strictly male at the time, our program was formally instituted under the Graduate School of Radcliffe. The very idea of women students at the graduate business school of Harvard was unheard of. We were not allowed to sit in on lectures with male students, so the Harvard professors came to us. One of my professors who seemed especially nervous later told me that he had to have a few martinis before each class because he was terrified of teaching women. How a male professor could be terrified of five nice women like my classmates and me, I do not understand.

I received straight A's in my classes. It was the first time in my educational experience that I had enough time to study, since I did not have to worry about finding a job and earning a living at the same time. My experience at Radcliffe gave me a great deal of confidence and an improved self-image: I was a success. The experimental management program for women at Radcliffe proved to be a success, too. It continued for twenty-five years, after which time women were finally admitted directly to Harvard Business School.

When I completed my studies, I had several job offers. One was with the YWCA (Young Women's Christian Association), but a professor who advised me said he did not think that it was the job for me. Another offer was as a representative for a lingerie manufacturing company where I would organize fashion shows. That job did not appeal to me. I returned to Los Angeles at the end of the 1937–1938 academic year, and looked for other opportunities. A professor of the Pasadena Junior College, whom I knew through a personnel association, said to me, "They're establishing a very interesting job in order to help young people find work, and you sound ideal for it." Through investigation, I learned that the superintendent of the Pasadena school system, which included the junior college, was working with the California employment office, the Chamber of Commerce and the Junior Chamber of Commerce to form a community-coordinated department that would focus entirely on the problems of young people in finding jobs.

The result was the Junior Counseling and Placement Department. The school system paid for one person—the director—who was to be in charge; the state of California provided the office and additional staff; the businesses, it was hoped, would provide the jobs. The program was the first of its kind in the United States.

When I applied for the position, the superintendent looked at my resumé and said, "Radcliffe is a pretty high class university. The kids in the Pasadena school system are poor. They don't get to a prestigious university like Radcliffe."

I replied: "I worked my way through college, sir," and described the many jobs I held to finance my education. Realizing I was a person who had participated in a life experience similar to that of the young people in the Pasadena school system, he immediately changed his view of me. I was the first person hired for the new department in Pasadena, and as its director I earned an annual salary of $1,800. I had assumed that my superiors would tell me what to do when I showed up for work, but they did not. The only guidance they gave me was: "You work it out." And so, I had to select the staff, organize the department, and establish the operating rules. This was the type of experience I enjoyed throughout my professional career.

I immediately set to work by selecting a psychologist who worked part-time to test the youths for ability, skills, and personality. Then, I had to decide the best approach to solving the problem of finding jobs for the area's young people. First, we tested all students who had signed up for the program to find out their capabilities; then I talked to them and counseled them. In each case, I asked: "What do you want to do?" Often, their idea of what they wanted to do had no relationship to their ability. The counseling session I had with each candidate was motivated by a desire to have the candidate work towards realistic goals. I tried to steer them in a direction that would make the most of their abilities.

I did the steering through my evaluations of their tests and their responses to my questions. I counseled them by recommending not only the goals that were feasible but the most rational means to attain those goals. I kept in close touch with the young people as they tried to get jobs, but even afterwards, they would often come back to the office to discuss their work. I consulted with the business people in the community and dealt mostly with presidents of firms. I spoke to meetings of the Junior and Senior Chamber of Commerce and found this link with the business community to be effective in getting results.

We recognized that the youngsters had no experience, and businesses quite properly did not see any advantage to hiring unqualified employees. I figured out how we could provide experience for the youngsters by recommending that the businesses hire these young people part-time initially in order to evaluate their performance. I helped to place thousands of youngsters in jobs. Most of the jobs, unfortunately, were for men, but I also succeeded in placing many women by persuading some business leaders to try out a woman in a job that had previously only been held by a man. I remember in particular a situation in which the largest department store in Pasadena hired only males for menial jobs. I told the president of the store, "Why don't you try out this young lady as a stockroom worker?"

He complied. Luckily, the woman was a magnificent employee. She was verbally superior to her male coworkers, made notes of things and kept good records, and introduced a better system of inventory control than the one that the store had been using. The president was pleased.

My interest in placing females into jobs was not motivated by any overt commitment to women's issues, as such. In this instance, women constituted a group of my clients. To serve them, I had to find jobs for them. When there were none, I tried to find openings for them in situations where only males had held jobs. In doing so, I discovered that it was easier to work directly with presidents than with personnel departments. My goal was to get the policy set. I recognized that if I convinced the president that what I was trying to do for young people was worthwhile, I had an entry right away. I would then go to the personnel director, who would follow the president's wishes. This procedure was far more effective than if I approached the personnel director first.

To help the program along, I recognized the importance of enlisting the media. Any time I wanted a story about some of these young people—and I had one about every week—the local newspaper, the *Pasadena Journal*, reported it. In this way, I was able to get a kind of community support which was wonderful. We were changing the rules in Pasadena about how young people could get jobs.

My job was great. I loved the young people and enjoyed working with company presidents. My boss, the superintendent of schools, was pleased with my performance. And I was being paid a decent salary for those times. With no thoughts of leaving, I had moved into my own apartment.

While I was working there, my brother Larry was living in Los Angeles with our mother and her second husband. He graduated from high school in June of 1941. Since I had been closer to him than to Evelyn and Dan, I was terribly concerned about his future. I designated myself as a sort of surrogate mother for him. We always kept in touch through correspondence and telephone, and we would visit each other often. I persuaded him that he had a wonderful opportunity at either West Point or the Naval Academy. I knew that if he was accepted, he wouldn't have the financial struggle that I had in getting my college degree since the U.S. government funded most of the educational costs. But being admitted was no easy matter. First, a candidate had to pass a written exam and then be nominated by a member of Congress. And finally, he (and at the time, it was always *he*) had to pass a physical examination.

Larry's grades in science and math were not good, so I persuaded him to attend Pasadena Junior College to improve his grades in those subjects. When this experience did not bring up his grades, I told him that I would pay $50 a month for him to attend a nearby preparatory school for a six-month period. At the time, I was making $150 a month. The prep school worked for Larry. When he took the written exam to become a cadet or midshipman, he placed first in southern California and was offered an appointment. I found a congressman from Pasadena who had a Naval Academy vacancy, and he sponsored my brother.

Just when I thought that everything was set, a navy doctor told Larry during his last physical exam that his eyesight was too poor for him to be admitted. Larry had had five previous eye examinations and passed with high grades. We both were heartbroken, and we cried. It was a devastating blow. I was still not ready to give up, however. Too much was at stake. I asked a friend of mine to recommend the name of a top civilian eye specialist in the Los Angeles area. Time was short, so when I called for an appointment I explained the circumstances. The appointment was scheduled for the next day, and the doctor concluded that my brother's eyes were perfect.

"Do you think the Naval Academy will accept your opinion?" I asked.

"I'm sure they will," he replied.

And yet, I wasn't sure because I didn't know anything about the Navy Department. I decided that I might as well begin at the top, and so I called the superintendent of the Naval Academy, Rear Admiral John R. Beardall. I introduced myself to the aide who answered the phone and explained the conflict between the opinion of the navy doctor and that of the civilian specialist regarding my brother's vision. The aide said that he would put the superintendent on the line. I described the situation to the superintendent, and then I said, "I am afraid that if my brother traveled to the Naval Academy, you might not accept him because of his eyes and we would both be very upset and heartbroken."

The admiral said in a very cordial voice: "Do you think that I, as superintendent of the Naval Academy, would have the nerve to turn down your brother, who has such a wonderful sister?"

That is the first time I had ever spoken to an admiral in the United States Navy. Little did I know that I would be speaking to other navy officers in the next few weeks and discussing matters which had nothing to do with my brother—but, rather, had everything to do with me.

two

WOMEN JOIN THE NAVY

While I was working in Pasadena, I was aware, like most Americans, of the dangerous international situation— particularly in Europe. After Germany invaded Poland in 1939 and World War II began in Europe, I paid more attention to overseas news than I had earlier. Although I was knowledgeable about the state of international affairs, I was not preoccupied with the subject. On December 7, 1941, I was in my apartment in Pasadena listening to the radio. At 8 A.M., I heard the shocking announcement about the attack on Pearl Harbor. The story told of the heavy toll of American lives and ships caused by the surprise Japanese military move. Americans could not believe the news: that our ships were sunk, and that Hickam airfield was a total disaster with planes on the ground on fire, and with personnel on the ground gunned down as they tried to get the planes in the air.

The story was just a horror; everybody was outraged. Living in California, I thought that we would be invaded next—a feeling shared by others living in the state. Americans felt so much fear that a blackout was established along the California coast. Alarm was heightened when one Japanese submarine reached the California shores and fired in daylight on a passenger train which ran between San Francisco and San Diego. Fortunately, it missed, but the incident increased our nervousness and anxiety about an all-out attack.

With the assault on Pearl Harbor, the United States was thrust into war against Japan. Japan's allies—Germany and Italy—then declared war against the United States. The conflict immediately became a war of truly global dimensions for which the United States was unprepared. Our nation had to mobilize quickly and on a large scale—developments that could only cause major consequences to the social, political, and economic fabric of American life.

The American people responded magnificently to the war. Many men signed up in the armed forces immediately—choosing not to wait to be drafted. Men and women sought to help the war effort at home as best they could. My feeling—and I believe that of every American—was shock at the treachery of the Japanese. The war immediately intruded on my life in a very direct way. A friend of mine working at a big army air corps[1] airfield in Riverside, California, wondered if I would double-date with her because she was bringing in a young lieutenant who had been called up from the reserves. She said, "He has a very attractive nice friend." I agreed to the double date.

My date turned out to be a delightful person, and I went out with him several times. About two months after I first met him, he received his orders to transfer to Pearl Harbor. Several weeks after his arrival there, he was sent to the forward area, where he was killed in action. His death was a real personal loss and brought the war very close to me. He was the first person I ever knew to die in the war. He was such a nice-looking, charming young man. I thought of him dying so young, and I was deeply saddened by his loss. One of the letters I had written him had been returned to me with a message stamped on the envelope: "Killed in Action."

I knew that before the war was over, many more young servicemen would die. I thought about how the war would affect the fate of my brothers. My younger brother Larry was applying to the Naval Academy. He would be serving the military in one way or another. My older brother Dan would not accept an army commission but enlisted instead. I never knew why, since he had a graduate degree, was married at the time, and deferred from military service.[2] Still, he voluntarily enlisted in the army. He was later to catch malaria when he was in the Pacific and New Guinea, and he suffered from the disease throughout his life.

Aside from these personal matters, I began to meet military people through my work. A few of them came to my office in Pasadena. They asked me to inform young men who came to see me about the need for young men in the military. I agreed both because it was the patriotic thing to do and because the military offered employment opportunities, which was the purpose for which my department had been established. The military men provided me with literature for distribution to the civilian youths who were unemployed. When my male clients came into the office, I informed them about the limited opportunities in the private sector and also about the kinds of jobs available in the armed services. But I also told them: "You should consider choosing a service rather than waiting to be drafted."

At the end of June 1942, Ada Comstock, the president of Radcliffe, called me to say that she was on the committee with the secretary of the navy considering the recruitment of women. The committee unanimously elected Mildred McAfee, the president of Wellesley, to be director of navy women. The women were advising the secretary of the navy, who in turn was talking with congressmen about the potential for women to serve and the need to pass enabling legislation for this purpose. President Comstock said: "There are going to be women—officers and enlisted—in the United States Navy. We are trying to get the top-notch women in the country. The officers will be college graduates; the enlisted will be high school graduates. I think you would be ideal. I think you would find serving in the navy exciting and the navy needs women with your experience."

In retrospect, I would like to think that I jumped at the opportunity for a pathbreaking career and the joy of contributing in a direct way to winning the war, but I did not. Because I knew nothing about the navy, I was not merely lukewarm to her request for me to join, I was actually chilly. What first came to my mind was what I later recognized to be the most trivial of considerations. "Do we have to wear a man's uniform?" I asked. My question was prompted by the only knowledge I had about the clothes of women in uniform: police women who wore a man's shirt, a man's tie, and a man's-style double-breasted jacket and trousers—all of which seemed to me inappropriate for women.

I did not want to dress like a man. I preferred feminine look-ing clothes. I was very *proud* of being a woman, a sentiment I had carried from my earliest years when my father made me feel it was a wonderful thing for me to be.

President Comstock dismissed my question about a uniform with the indifference it deserved. "Oh, I don't know anything about that," she replied. "I would like you to go down to see the navy people. I have already written them a letter about you."

I wanted to say "No," but I couldn't, not to Ada Comstock. She was a very distinguished woman and an important person in my life. I had too much respect for her not to do what she asked of me.

"I've already talked to them about you," she said. "So you call and make an appointment. The bill permitting women in the navy has not been passed in Congress yet, but it is pending. There is no question that the bill is going to be passed. And so, I would like you to go down and be ready to be commissioned."

I did not have the slightest doubt that the prospect of wearing a male-looking uniform—awful as that would be for me—would prevent me from complying with any request from President Comstock. I made an appointment at the Naval Procurement Of-fice in Los Angeles (the recruitment location for naval officers), just as she had asked me to do. When I went there in July, I faced one man in uniform with a broad gold stripe on his sleeve, and a number of women dressed in civilian clothes—all seated around a large table. I was told privately that the officer was an admiral. I think the women were deans or presidents of women's colleges. They questioned me about many matters, although they already knew all about me from President Comstock. One of the women asked me: "Will you take the physical? Everyone in the military must be physically fit."

"If I take the physical, am I automatically in the navy?" I asked. They assured me that the taking of the physical would not mean that I was in the navy and that they would discuss later what rank would be offered me. I took the physical the next day and passed. When I returned to the room to meet the selection committee, one of the women said: "What would you like to be?"

"I don't understand your question."

"What *rank* would you like to be?"

I was perplexed. "Since I know nothing about the United States Navy, I think that you're a better judge of that than I am." As I told the story years later, I said, "You know if you're stupid, you end up as an ensign." I was commissioned an ensign in the U.S. Navy five days after the law was passed.

I soon learned that a commission is an appointment from the president of the United States to be an officer in the U.S. military. A navy commission carries a rank, and the lowest rank is ensign. The ranks then rise to lieutenant jg (junior grade), lieutenant, lieutenant commander, commander, captain, commodore (only used in wartime), rear admiral, vice admiral, and admiral. An additional wartime title of fleet admiral is used for an admiral commanding ships, planes, and men in combat in a specific area.

Events moved quickly. On July 30, 1942, the law permitting women in the navy reserve was passed. On August 4 in Los Angeles, I was commissioned, one day after Mildred McAfee had received her commission as lieutenant commander and had been sworn in as director of the WAVES. She was in Washington, D.C., at the time. My commission ceremony was similar to that of my male officer counterparts with one exception. In "normal" cases, a mid-ranged officer administers the oath of office to support the United States. But mine was not a normal case. For me, the admiral who had been at the table when I was first interviewed for the navy administered the oath while I faced him and raised my right hand.

The admiral read these words: "He is therefore carefully and diligently to discharge the duties of such office. . . . And I do strictly charge and require all officers, seamen, and marines under his command to be obedient to his orders. And he is therefore to follow such orders and directions from time to time as he shall receive from me, or the future president of the United States, or his superior officer assigned to him. . . ." The ceremony and commission took no notice of my gender. After I had recited the oath, the admiral congratulated me and told me that I was now an officer of the United States Navy. "As a commissioned officer," he said, "you are to follow the high standards of the navy and behave as an officer and gentleman." I thought to myself that I would behave as an officer, but I had no idea of how I would behave as a gentleman.

After the swearing-in ceremony, the admiral informed me that I would receive orders and a transportation voucher for train fare to report to the U.S. Naval Training School at Smith College in Northampton, Massachusetts, on August 28, 1942, for one month's training. He said he would request that upon completion of my training, I be ordered back to his office to assist in the selection of additional women officers. Then he offered me his congratulations on becoming one of the first women officers in the U.S. Navy.

Maybe I would have been less complacent about my assignment had I known that in wartime more than in peacetime, one cannot even be moderately certain about future assignments.

Ensign Winifred Quick leaves Pasadena, California, in August 1942, to commence one month's training at the U.S. Naval School, Smith College.

⚓ ⚓ ⚓

In some respects, the practice of including women in the military in World War II was not a new development in U.S. military experience. A few women secretly dressed like men to fight in the American Revolutionary War and in wars that followed, and women later participated in a formally recognized manner. It can be argued that women's participation goes back to 1813 when two women were listed in the ship's log of the frigate *United States* as supernumerary crew members. In 1862, nurses went aboard the navy's first hospital ship, the U.S.S. *Red Rover*. In 1908, the U.S. Navy Nurse Corps was established, and twenty nurses became the first "official" women in the navy. During World War I, women served as yeoman (F)[3] but they were never made a formal part of the U.S. Naval Reserve or U.S. Marine Corps Reserve. Women served as navy nurses in World War I, too, but were not commissioned as officers. When the war ended, the enlisted navy women were discharged.

It was World War II which led to the breakthrough for women's participation in the military, made necessary by the demands of building up a huge military and industrial establishment composed of a fighting force and supporting units as well. More than their earlier counterparts, the modern armed services of World War II required the use of an astonishing variety of talents—more skills even than those demanded by all of the biggest industrial enterprises combined. For now, unlike any other time in the nation's history, the United States was fighting a global war. The armed forces required the talents of chemists, physicists, mathematicians, engineers, scientists, doctors, nurses, medical and military technicians, lawyers, administrators, clothing designers, real estate experts, and many other professional people, skilled workers, and manual laborers. Moreover, in addition to needing a larger and more sophisticated military establishment, the United States needed civilians to build ships, design aircraft, manufacture guns, produce uniforms, and otherwise support the fighting forces. It was clear by early 1942 that the U.S. government would have to tap every material and human resource it could to win the war against its formidable foes.

The assessment of human resources by senior civilian and military leaders established the need for women to play a vital role in the war effort—both in civilian and military tasks. In the civilian sector, women replaced many men in factory jobs and other positions. Perhaps the most engaging model of the times was that of "Rosie the Riveter"—a woman holding a quintessential man's job. Both men and women applauded women's involvement in the civilian war effort and their performance in jobs that were traditionally regarded as reserved for men. Women who accepted these jobs were true patriots. After all, everybody was expected to pitch in. If you weren't doing something to help win the war, either in a volunteer role or a full-time civilian or military job, most Americans believed you weren't a good citizen.

When civilian and military leaders realized that mobilizing all available manpower resources would still not give the United States all the personnel it needed for its armed forces, they turned to *woman*power. They understood that women could help not only by working at civilian tasks but also by working directly for the military establishment. In the fall of 1941, the army established the Women's Army Auxiliary Corps (WAAC).[4] On July 30, 1942, the Naval Reserve Act of 1938 was amended by Public Law 689 to include the women's reserve (later known as WAVES), which authorized women officers and enlisted women to serve in the navy. The WAVES, established as a component of the naval reserve, initially served "to release a man to fight at sea."

The plan at that time was to recruit 11,000 women, but so great were the demands for "manpower" that in less than a year this initial purpose had become outmoded. The need for greatly expanded naval forces on and under the sea and in the air made it expedient to use more and more women to staff navy stations ashore. No longer would the WAVES mission be simply to release a man to fight at sea, but instead to work side by side with men as a regular part of the navy staff. The number of women in the WAVES increased constantly throughout the war. By the time of Japan's surrender, 86,000 WAVES were serving their country.

Like the men who flocked to recruiting centers soon after Pearl Harbor, the women who volunteered for the WAVES joined up for the most part because of patriotism and a strong desire to help the war effort. When opportunities became available for women in the military, women recognized that they, too, could serve their country. Moreover, unlike the men, the women were under no legal obligation for military service, so their volunteering was not in response to the fear of being drafted. The reserve volunteers who joined the WAVES committed themselves "for the duration and six months"—that is to say, for whatever time it took to defeat the enemy nations plus six months—the same commitment that the male reservists made. Throughout the war the WAVES—like the male reservists—regarded themselves as temporary, full-time workers who expected to return to civilian life once the war was over.

A distinguishing feature for the WAVES, which made it unique among other women's organizations in the U.S. military in World War II, was its status as a part of the U.S. Navy Reserves. In contrast, women in the army's WAACs were a separate corps. With the establishment of the WAVES, the navy became the first military service to give commissions to women officers. Navy women, both officers and enlisted personnel, were subject to many of the same regulations as navy men, but there were differences too. In 1942–1943, women in the navy were subject to different housing regulations. They could not be married, could not serve if they had children, and would be discharged if they became pregnant.

The granting of commissions to women was an important first step in the progress that women were going to achieve in the decades ahead. Equally important was the fact that the navy established the principle from the very beginning that women would receive pay equal to the rank or rating of their male counterparts. For example, the pay for a female lieutenant (jg) was the same as for a male lieutenant (jg), and an enlisted woman received the same pay as her male counterpart. When we realize that income disparity for women performing the same tasks as men in the civilian sector in 1942 (and in decades to come!) was the rule rather than the exception, we can see that the navy was truly a trailblazer in granting equal pay for equal work. Because navy officials declined to make navy women an auxiliary force, the women officers and enlisted were assured equality of income with their navy male counterparts.

In many respects other than pay, however, the navy was similar to the other military services in its sexist attitude toward job assignments for women. These attitudes impeded the progress of women in the military and hindered the overall effectiveness of the women's arm of the military as well. These sexist attitudes were not unique to the navy or the other services, but rather were based on attitudes prevalent throughout American society. In civilian occupations, women tended to hold subservient jobs rather than leadership positions.

The development of the WAVES was influenced not only by the legislation providing for its organization, role, and status but by considerations based on experience as well. During the development stage, most organizations must make decisions about the adoption of fundamental procedures and rules based on expectations rather than on past history. The women's naval reserve—and the male navy leaders, too—had to begin its work with few precedents to guide it through decisions about uniforms, promotions, pregnancy policy, marriage policy, training, housing, discipline, and assignments. Some of these decisions could be based on existing legislation and regulations, but others had to be improvised based on a variety of factors, including the demands of war, experience with existing rules, judgment about the consequences of specific policies, prevailing attitudes by men about women, and cultural and social standards.

A key decisionmaker in 1942 was Mildred McAfee, who consulted and advised senior navy officers about policies concerning women in the navy. She played an extraordinarily important role in determining such matters as how women should be treated compared to men and what kinds of assignments women would take, as well as housing conditions, supervision, and discipline standards. She wisely yielded to the use of the term WAVES when the *Washington Post* reported in August 1942 as part of a story about women in the naval reserve that the women "goblets" were coming to town—the term *gobs* being the slang word for male enlisted naval personnel. She did not want any disparaging term—formal or informal—used for the navy women.

Lieutenant Commander McAfee helped avoid many disasters for women of the navy. She was a born diplomat who handled her discussions with the senior officers with great finesse, as the following story suggests. Admiral Randall Jacobs, the chief of naval personnel, suggested to her that he thought navy women would look smashing in black stockings like those of the Women's Royal Naval Service (Wrens), the British counterpart of the WAVES. The black stockings of 1942 were not the sensuous hosiery that designers of women's clothes create in the 1990s, but instead were unattractive cotton and rayon stockings that sagged around the knees and ankles.[5] McAfee never revealed the shock she felt about the idea, instead saying to Admiral Jacobs: "What a brilliant idea, Admiral. I never would have thought of it myself." Two days later she told him she had contacted several hosiery manufacturers who had explained to her that since civilian women did not wear black stockings, the navy would have to pay considerably more for them than for the colored stockings normally worn.

"Admiral Jacobs," she said, "our navy women are very patriotic and are perfectly willing to wear the same color hosiery as civilian women." Jacobs accepted the economic logic and the appeal to love of country, so the idea of black stockings received its proper demise.

Providentially, I think, the navy commissioned the American designer Main Rousseau Bocher, who owned the fashion house of Mainbocher, to create a uniform for the WAVES. It wanted a "classy" image to reflect a special group of educated, prestigious women. The result was a uniform which was closely identified with the traditional navy and yet was feminine as well. Included in the uniform was a hat—a traditional component of all military uniforms. We did not have double-breasted suits like the navy men, which are unattractive on women. Instead, we had short, fitted navy-blue jackets with padded shoulders, rounded collars, pointed lapels, and matching gored skirts. Our blouses were blue at first (and later, white), and our black ties—unlike a man's— were knotted to form a bow. The navy provided coordinating black shoulder purses as part of the uniform, plus black pumps or lace shoes for enlisted women.

Outside of the obvious need to make female officers' uniforms different from their male officer counterparts, there were two other interesting differences in the uniforms. First, in choosing "navy blue" as a color, the navy varied the color of its traditional uniforms. Male officers in the navy wore uniforms which looked black but were dark navy blue. Second, the officer rank, indicated on the jacket sleeve, was not made of gold thread, as was the case with uniforms of male officers, but rather of a lighter shade of blue braid sewn on the jacket sleeve. I don't recall that either of these differences made us feel like second-class citizens. We were very proud of our WAVE uniforms.

The uniforms came as a great surprise to me and my classmates in basic training. We received them the day before we graduated after four weeks of training, and as soon as they arrived, we were fitted and the necessary alterations were made. We made our first appearance in uniform on graduation, much to the de-

Graduation of the first class of navy women officers, September 1942. Official U.S. Navy photograph.

light of our civilian audience, some of whom were Smith and Mt. Holyoke students who later signed up for duty. We women officers and the enlisted loved those uniforms, as did the public. My earlier concern about wearing a man's uniform vanished the moment we received our attractive, feminine Mainbocher designs.

When some of my fellow WAVE officers and I went to New York City soon after the uniforms were issued to us, we were greeted with applause by an admiring public. Even the admiral who had been on my procurement board at the Naval Procurement Office in Los Angeles wrote to me and asked: "How do you like the uniform now?" I wrote him an enthusiastic reply.

The navy publicized the uniform by noting its stylish appearance and mentioning the fact that the famous Mainbocher was its designer. According to the rules of the time, women were given an allowance of $200 for clothing. The official uniform consisted of "everything that shows" except shoes, purse, and gloves. The cost—about $160—was paid for from the $200 allowance. The balance of about $40 was provided for shoes, underclothing, and anything else that the officer or recruit needed.

The enlisted women's uniform was identical to the officers' except for the hat, which was unfortunately both impractical (it blew away easily in the wind) and unattractive (the enlisted women hated it). Soon that hat was discontinued and another one (called an overseas hat), both more practical and more attractive, took its place. The ratings of enlisted women (yeoman, etc.) were signified by a special device worn on the upper left sleeve. For the enlisted women the special device indicated occupational specialty (i.e., yeoman, storekeeper). Both officers and enlisted wore two light blue anchors on the lapel of their uniforms.

⚓ ⚓ ⚓

The WAVES had to receive training. All I knew on August 4, 1942, was that on August 28, I had to report to the commanding officer, Training Headquarters for Women, which, as mentioned, was at Smith College, in Northampton, Massachusetts.[6] Smith was the first women naval officers' training school. For me, my assignment there meant taking a train trip across the country. En route to Smith, I stopped at the Naval Academy in Annapolis, Maryland, to visit my brother Larry. He was surprised to see me. Since he was only a plebe, which by naval tradition is the lowest form of humanity, he was impressed when I told him I was an ensign.

"An ensign is God around here," he said. "Walk with me down the path. Don't hold my hand. Don't sit on the bench. They'll never believe that you're my sister. You'll get me in all kinds of trouble, so please be careful." His concern was motivated by the fact that plebes were subject to strict rules and were prohibited from having a girl friend on the Academy grounds. With each offense came a demerit with punishment.

On August 28, I arrived at Smith College with 119 other women who were the first commissioned women in the U.S. Navy. We were met at the station and taken to our quarters in one of the dormitories, which had been contracted from Smith College for use by naval personnel. Late in the day, we gathered in a large room to be greeted by our commanding officer, Captain Herbert W. Underwood, an Academy graduate recalled from retired status. The navy had conducted many interviews just to pick this one very important officer. Flexible, adaptable, and imaginative, he proved to be superb for the job and assumed his responsibility with real enthusiasm. Other navy men were less enthusiastic—even hostile—to the idea of women in the navy, so the appointment of Captain Underwood was crucial to getting the program underway successfully.

During the next thirty days, all of the women officers at Smith went through physical examinations even though we had taken physicals a few weeks earlier. We received a full line-up of inoculations identical to the shots that our male officer counterparts received, including shots for tetanus, smallpox, and typhoid. The medics hit both arms in one day, and we accepted this procedure with mixed emotions but no complaints.

The population of this class was much smaller than later classes would be, because the navy wanted to get the first class through quickly so that its graduates could help take responsibility for future classes and could perform other jobs in procurement throughout the United States. My classmates came from all over the country and consisted of scientists, teachers, administrators, and business people. All of them had college degrees, and some had advanced degrees. Religious affiliations varied, but racial backgrounds did not—a situation that took years to change.

One of our first difficult adjustments was learning to live with a much more compressed and confining housing situation than most of us were used to. We were assigned four women to a room. We had double bunks, no pillows, no dressers, no desks, no chairs, very few bathrooms, and very little privacy. We did have plenty of New England humidity and hot weather—there was no air conditioning in 1942. I was lucky that the housing officer gave me an upper bunk, since the lower bunk was almost on the floor.

Another adjustment was military life itself. Reveille was at 5:30 A.M. and muster at 6:00 A.M. We had breakfast at 6:30 A.M. Our instructors were an all-male group of reserve officers—ensigns, lieutenant (jgs), and a few full lieutenants—who were in actuality only two steps ahead of us in these early months of American involvement in World War II because they had just recently been called to active duty. Unfortunately, we did not have textbooks and depended almost entirely on the lectures to gain knowledge of naval subjects. Without textbooks, and with only a short time to learn so many new facts, we had great difficulty in retaining the information. There was much uncertainty about what "training" was supposed to mean. We knew it meant at the minimum learning basic facts about the navy. Our instructors gave us lectures on military protocol (which included teaching us how to salute), identification of ships and aircraft, and navy history, customs, and traditions. We learned to distinguish an officer's rank.

While all naval officers—regardless of gender—are supposed to undergo educational training to teach them basic facts about the navy, the physical part of the training was different. The women did not have to perform the kind of rigorous, physical exercises that their male counterparts had to endure. Still, it was clear that navy women had to learn how to march.

The instructors for our physical exercises and marching arrived one day in early September, straight out of central casting. All over six feet tall, the men were part of a physical fitness program trained by former boxing champion Gene Tunney to be muscle builders. The women—diminutive compared to them— looked upon them as giants. The navy had given Tunney a commission in hopes that he would encourage strong, husky men to join the service. The navy used these strong men at its male training schools.

Our giants tried to teach us how to march. At first, we wore civilian clothes and tennis shoes in our marching since our WAVES uniforms had not yet arrived. From the point of view of our trainers, we were not physically conditioned to march. Where they took gargantuan steps—a practice standard for them—we took our normal steps—which turned up short. After one day of our trying to match their mammoth steps, Captain Underwood said: "No way." And so, the Tunney instructors were sent back to Washington.

Captain Underwood devised an impromptu solution to our problem of learning how to march. Towards the end of our month's training period, we had one of our own women officers who had been in physical education in civilian life become our marching instructor. This practice worked so well that in future classes women who had been physical education teachers in civilian life provided physical training and marching to the WAVES.

I never did learn how to march—unlike some of the other women. I would go along with the marches when I had to but I surely never knew how to call orders nor, fortunately, was I ever called on to do so.

For all of our military appearance, the first class of WAVES at Smith had a relatively easy time of things as we were less regimented than classes that came after us. We were not really regimented because it took some time for the navy to set up the regimentation routines. For example, we didn't have to march down to our evening meals, as was the practice for the next and subsequent navy training classes at Smith. We could go down to meals in groups or singly.

One of our unanticipated joys was the meals. We had them at the Wiggins Tavern, a famous hotel and restaurant renowned for its service and gourmet food. In fact, the tavern was rated as a four-star restaurant in civilian life.

The navy had taken over the entire facility—including the hotel rooms. It was located several blocks from Smith. The regular tavern employees were under contract to the navy, so we were assured gourmet food and magnificent service at every single meal. The tavern (called an officer's mess) had a bar, and cocktails were available at dinner. It was gracious living. Although officers paid for their meals out of their food allowance, the price was extremely low. This dining part of the Smith experience was very pleasant. And to think, the navy called its dining facilities a "mess"!

I was pleased to meet many fine women in that first class at Smith. Since my life had been marked by constant change and travel, I did not feel that I had to adapt very much to new influences. Still, some women adjusted better to the navy than I did. In their case, their adjustment was easier than mine because they had been eager to join up for military service, while I was a bit reluctant.

Service in the military moved most women from one social environment to an entirely new one. Sometimes, this change produced amusing consequences, as was the case with one of my classmates, Ensign Winifred Love. She had been raised in a very strict Presbyterian family, and navy life was an exciting adventure for her. Once I asked Winifred if she'd like to join me for dinner at the officer's mess, and she was delighted. As we sat down, I asked her what she'd like to drink. "I don't know, because I've never had a drink," she said.

"Well, I'll have to think of something mild," I commented, whereupon I ordered two martinis.

When dinner time approached the next night, she was waiting for me with a question: "Can we go to dinner again and have that same mild drink?"

Towards the end of the training period, each member of the class received her assignment for the next post. A great many women went off to distant places throughout the United States.

The admiral in Los Angeles had told me that I would return to his office where I could recruit women officers. When the orders came out on September 28, I learned that I would not be going to California as I had thought. I was shocked to discover that I was assigned to remain at the Naval Officer School at Smith College.

When I told Captain Underwood that I felt my orders were incorrect, he said: "It's all my fault. I had your orders changed because I wanted you here for personnel work. Why don't you come over to my office? We'll talk it over."

I went over to his office but my fate was sealed. I knew I couldn't have my orders changed. Captain Underwood had spoken to my class as a group but never to me privately. By this time, I knew that a captain was at a very high rank because he had four stripes.

"With your personnel background," he said, "you will be very useful here because we have 700 women officer candidates who are reporting here in two weeks. I would like you to tell me what to do with them. I want you to be my personnel director. You've already had a very fine background in that field. I know nothing about women."

"But Captain, Sir," I said.

"You can either call me 'Captain' or 'Sir'—not both," he interrupted. I knew so little about navy protocol at the time that I did not even know how to address a superior officer properly.

"I know nothing about the navy," I said in alarm.

"That's the beauty of it," he remarked. "We're going to work as a team. I know the navy; you know personnel matters."

At the time, I did not know that the idea of an ensign and a captain working as a team was an unusual situation in the navy. I asked: "Could I go and think about this? Because I've got to make plans, and I will need at least six interviewers."

"I knew you'd say that," he replied and walked away.

I was in a state of shock. Not only wouldn't I be going to California as I had expected, but now I was being asked to interview 700 probationary officers coming in two weeks. It was a tough job. I would have to select and train a staff and outline our procedures as well as develop forms to record the women's abilities, their civilian skills, their personal preferences, and their personality traits. I returned to Captain Underwood and he arranged to fulfill my requests—including finding the officers I needed for my staff and the furniture to use in our work. My office was at the beautiful alumni building at Smith, which the navy had taken over for its staff.

The new job made many more demands of me than I had experienced at either of my previous personnel positions. The responsibilities were greater and my deadline was shorter. It was like accelerating in a quantum leap from five miles per hour to a hundred miles per hour.

"This is the way I will work," I told Captain Underwood. "I'll divide the staff of six into three teams of two interviewers each. I want each team to interview about one-third of the probationary officers. I need three teams because we have such a short space of time to interview the women. In fairness to the candidates—all of whom are prestigious, professional women—I'd like two opinions on each of them. If the opinions of the interviewers don't coincide fairly closely, I'll interview them and make a final decision."

Captain Underwood said that this method of interviewing the women was excellent, so he endorsed my proposed procedures. My work consisted of running the entire operation. I had to supervise my staff of interviewers and hold staff meetings with them to sharpen our techniques. To some extent the work I was doing was similar to my civilian job in Pasadena, except that there, I knew what jobs the employer wanted. At Smith, I had no idea what jobs navy women would fill. All we could do was to evaluate their civilian experience and record it. The navy was not derelict in telling me what jobs they needed the women officers to perform, because in 1942 nobody within the navy knew what work the women or men officers in the reserve were supposed to do.

Since there were no precedents to draw upon, the interviewer ensigns and I had to improvise by coming up with our own solutions to these problems. We had to design questions that would reveal enough information about each probationary officer to determine her personality, her previous skills and work experience, and her educational background. The entire interview had to be conducted in ten minutes. Pressure was terrific; yet we wanted to do a good job for these outstanding women.

Although I conducted few interviews, I made certain that all of the reports were sent to me. I went over every one of them to see if there was enough information to allow somebody to make a decision about where to place the officer candidate. The three teams of interviewers consisted of six ensigns whom I picked from my class at Smith. They worked very effectively, and disagreements about evaluating any candidate were rare. They were a superb and dedicated staff. When the second training facility for WAVES opened at Mount Holyoke College, which was located a few miles away in neighboring South Hadley, Massachusetts, I ran the personnel program there as well as at Smith. My work involved evaluation of the skills for women officers but not for enlisted personnel.

Two months after I was appointed personnel director, Captain Underwood said to me: "It is traditional in the navy that a department head can't be the same rank as the subordinates. I have recommended that you be spot-promoted to lieutenant (jg)." The recommendation was approved, and I was promoted. Spot-promotion was an unusual step in the navy since the typical practice was to give promotions based on time in a rank, fitness reports, and record. In a normal situation, such a promotion would take several years, but World War II was not a normal situation.

As a department head, I was given a housing perk. I moved from the dormitory to Clarke House, a residential house at Smith which had far better facilities than the dormitories. Clarke House became the home of the senior staff members—that is to say, the department heads. I now shared quarters with six other staff members, with each room containing only two women officers. I appreciated how much more livable Clarke House was than the dormitory. We even had a guest room with a private bath, which we named the Eleanor Roosevelt Room in honor of the First Lady whom we all admired.

Lieutenant (jg) Winifred Redden Quick, USNR, proudly displays her new rank. She was spot promoted after three months active duty as director, Officer Personnel, Naval Training School (Smith College), November 1942. Official U.S. Navy photograph.

When my midshipman brother Larry visited me during Christmas of 1942, he was overcome by the luxury of his room at Clarke House. He was also surprised to hear, each morning and evening, hundreds of women midshipmen singing as they marched by en route to the mess hall. Of course, the midshipmen at Annapolis sang while they marched, too. But Larry was astonished to learn that navy women did the same thing. Although music and singing had always been part of navy culture, navy women took it up with great gusto. In 1942, officers at Smith and Mt. Holyoke established a woman's choir, directed by Ensign Ruthanna Maxwell. Her view was that "singing people are essentially happy

Winifred Quick and her brother, Midshipman Larry S. Redden, USN, a
Naval Academy plebe, during his visit
to the Officer Training School at Smith
College in December 1942.

people." The WAVES had a song for everything. As Maxwell described music for the WAVES at this time: "When something good
happens, when something not so pleasant comes along, when
swinging up from drill on a glowing autumn day, when struggling
on the icy hills to class on a bitter Saturday morning, when sitting
waiting, just waiting in a line, somewhere in the ranks, a song
starts and grows and swells in volume until all are singing."[7]

The choir sang at nearby colleges and on radio broadcasts. Its
most popular song was "I Need a Guy to Tie My Tie," but perhaps
the song which captured the spirit of the WAVES was this one,
which was sung first when I was at Smith.

WAVES of the Navy
There's a ship sailing down the bay
And she won't slip into port again
Until that Victory Day.
Carry on for that gallant ship
And for every hero brave
Who will find ashore, his man-sized chore
Was done by a navy WAVE.

According to Maxwell, no single person was the author of the song's lyrics. It was composed by a group of WAVES. "It just happened," she says.[8] The WAVES choir became an institution and continued even after World War II ended. It featured some magnificent voices.[9]

During the twelve months I was there, the entire WAVES operation at Smith College was beginning to take on a more regulated structure than was the case when I first arrived there. We now had department heads for each phase of the program: medical, instruction, fitting of uniforms, physicals, exercise, and drill. Each educational subject was now taught by a different instructor, and all students now had navy texts!

Although navy women were volunteers, they had to follow orders. Rules were rigorously enforced. One beautiful blond, a WAVE ensign of the second class at Smith, was court-martialed because she left her duty post for a bit of frivolity. Each month some women were sent home because they couldn't cope with the physical and psychological challenges. Another challenge was dealing with the climate. For example, the winter of 1942–1943 set a record in Massachusetts for low temperatures. Ordinarily, we were kept warm by the Mainbocher suits, the heavy lined overcoats, and comfortable hats. The best protection we had was the glamorous havelock that fitted over our hat and fell to our shoulders, making us appear as if we belonged to the French foreign legion. All the WAVES loved the look.

Regardless of this protection, not all WAVES could deal with the cold weather of this particular winter. A half-dozen southern women, accustomed to a warm climate, suffered frostbite. They benefited from their discomfort, however, because they were relieved of the necessity of marching until they thawed out and healed. They were transported to their classes in station wagons and waved and smiled as they passed.

WAVES officers at Smith were privileged to meet some of the nation's most illustrious people. In addition to Eleanor Roosevelt, whose visit will be discussed later, we often met with Mrs. Calvin Coolidge, the widow of the president, who taught for many years at a school for the hearing impaired at Northampton. She was a great friend of the WAVES. Mrs. Coolidge graciously loaned her lovely Northampton home to Captain and Mrs. Underwood. Writers Dorothy Parker and Sinclair Lewis shared a nightcap with the WAVES in Northampton in the Wiggins Tavern after she gave a speech. The women were most curious about the relationship of the two celebrities.

In my year at Smith, I found the community—both at the college and in town—to be most hospitable to the WAVES. We mixed well with the students and faculty. Some of the students so admired the WAVES that upon graduation, they signed up. The students were hospitable to the WAVES in so many ways in spite of the fact that we had five of their finest buildings and had taken over Wiggins Tavern.

⚓ ⚓ ⚓

Although my work as personnel director at the WAVES officer schools did not include enlisted recruits, I was aware in the fall of 1942 of the desperate need for trained enlisted personnel and the top priority placed on the immediate need for recruitment of enlisted women. Although there were enlisted specialty schools in operation for training male enlisted men, these schools were filled to capacity and there was no room for enlisted WAVES.

The Navy Department appealed to numerous university administrations to provide space for training enlisted women. Several universities offered classrooms, housing, dining facilities, and outdoor areas for physical and marching training. The first of these were Oklahoma A&M at Stillwater and Iowa State Teachers College at Cedar Falls, for teaching yeomen; the University of Wisconsin for the teaching of storekeepers; and the University of Indiana for the teaching of radio operators. WAVE officers in the first class at Smith College were rushed to staff these colleges, as the deadline for opening operations was October 9, 1942. Since no recruit school (boot camp) had yet been established, the instructions at these academic institutions included military indoctrination as well as the specialty training. A few of the top yeomen who had previously worked for leading corporate executives were rushed to senior admirals in the Navy Department. The admirals were absolutely astounded at the intelligence and expertise of these brand new women yeomen. They quickly demanded that more enlisted women be recruited.

As a result of the demand for more enlisted WAVES, two schools for storekeepers were opened at the Victoria Hotel in Boston and one at the Naval Training School at Milledgeville, Georgia. Miami University in Florida responded with facilities for a training school for radio operators. As mounting numbers of casualties in World War II created an urgency for WAVE hospital corpsmen, by February 1, 1943, nine schools were opened at naval hospitals across the country.

On February 17, 1943, Hunter College, a nonresident civilian college in the Bronx, New York, was commissioned as the U.S. Naval Training School for WAVE enlisted personnel. It had transportation advantages as well as adequate space for training. Since it had no dormitories, the navy commandeered adjacent apartment buildings. Hundreds of double-deck bunks were installed to house the new recruits. The mayor of New York City had given his blessing and cooperation by finding apartments for the tenants who were dislodged. Hunter College (the boot camp for women recruits) had a population of 6,000–7,000 at one time. During the course of World War II, 80,350 WAVES, 1,844 Coast Guard, and 3,190 marines were trained there. Hunter was receiving 2,000 recruits every two weeks.[10]

As the needs of the war expanded, the enlisted WAVES soon had a wider array of assignments for which they could qualify. Some of these assignments were the kinds of work that women would traditionally do in civilian jobs, such as bookkeeper, typist, commercial artist, receptionist, librarian, and hairdresser. But women could also receive training and assignments in roles that had previously been held exclusively by men, not only in the military establishment but in civilian society as well. Among these jobs were cartographer, aerologist, parachute rigger, radio technician, lithographer, link trainer, and electrician.[11] At war's end a few WAVES held some unusual jobs. One was pigeonman (a trainer of homing pigeons that would be used by lighter-than-airship crews for communications during radio silence while seeking enemy submarines). Ensign Ruthanna Maxwell told me in January 1943 about her Mount Holyoke class in cryptography, the art of writing in secret character codes. The last lecture in her class before the commissioning was called the "scare" lecture, in which students were told horrifying stories of what had happened when errors were made in the code room. When it was learned that the enemy had broken a particular code, it had to be deleted from the program. It was WAVE officers who went to Boston to the navy yard and obtained the new codes to be taught. "Who would ever suspect a woman was responsible for transporting such important material?" Ensign Maxwell asked. "Not many people in those days."

While stationed at Great Lakes Naval Station for field work in the code room, she had her first experience with what later became the title of a classroom lecture—"Miss Maxwell's Experience with a Spy." She had been visiting the Chicago Art Institute and was on a train back to Highland Park in Illinois. A young man sat down beside her and started a conversation. As the chat progressed, she noticed he was asking pertinent questions, including: "How many WAVES are stationed at Great Lakes?" "Where do they live?" "What are they doing?" "What is a communications job like?" She soon realized that she had a problem—or thought she did. When she left the train at her usual stop, she reported her experience to the Security Office at Great Lakes, and they were able to remove the man from the train for questioning. She was never told the outcome of the investigation, however.[12]

⚓ ⚓ ⚓

When the women midshipmen completed their training, they were commissioned officers and assigned to shore activities which required them to work side by side with male officers. They did the same work as their male counterparts.

Although I had no role in making assignments to shore activities for WAVE officers, I did have a role in selecting their WAVE officer supervisors. I also played a role in asking WAVE officers if they wished to volunteer for the SPARS[13] (the Coast Guard women's reserve) or the marines. Women had volunteered for the Coast Guard and the marines for the same reason they had volunteered for the navy—because of patriotism and the desire to help win the war. SPARS was formed in November of 1942, nearly four months after the women's naval reserve had been established. Women entered the marines in March 1943. I interviewed WAVE volunteers for either the SPARS or the marines and passed on the personnel data from our interviews to the marines and Coast Guard.

In December 1942, twelve WAVES were selected as SPARS and resigned their WAVE commissions to join that organization.

Later, nineteen WAVES resigned their commissions to accept commissions in the U.S. Marine Corps. The first officers for the SPARS and for the women's marine reserve had gone through training at Smith and Mt. Holyoke. The Coast Guard even selected one woman—Dorothy Stratton—from the class I attended at Smith and named her director of the SPARS. She had been dean of women and a professor of psychology at Purdue University. In 1943, the Coast Guard and the marines selected their own officers and established their own programs.

As the navy tried to increase the number of women volunteers in the WAVES, it discovered that many women were not joining because of the policy against marriage. Since this restric-

The first marriage of a WAVES officer took place at Smith College in April, 1943, when Ensign Shirley Bailey married Ensign Fred Maiwurm. Navy regulation permitted the bride to wear a civilian wedding dress but the groom, if he was military, was required to wear his uniform. Official U.S. Navy photograph.

tion proved to be a hindrance to the recruitment of women, the navy repealed the regulation in 1943. The first marriage of a WAVES officer took place at Smith College on April 6, 1943, and I attended that ceremony. Navy regulation permitted the bride to wear a civilian wedding dress for the ceremony and reception but the groom—if he was in the military—was required to wear his uniform. After the ceremony and reception, the bride had to return to wearing a uniform as the regulations did not permit civilian clothing to be worn beyond the ceremony.

During wartime, a married WAVE and her military husband recognized that in all likelihood they would not spend the war years together, as it was impossible to make special efforts to assign a husband and wife to the same place. But in World War II, a person in the military expected to be separated from his or her spouse even if the latter were a civilian. Consequently, there was nothing unique about a married WAVE living away from her husband. If the officer or enlisted WAVE got pregnant, then she was required to be released from the service with an honorable discharge. The same rule applied to unmarried women who became pregnant.

One woman who married during her tour of duty was Ensign Maxwell (now Mrs. Ruthanna Weber). She had to get permission for leave. The purpose for leave read "Matrimony." Captain Underwood noted in his own handwriting at the bottom of the page: "Purpose duly noted. Unchartered waters—proceed with caution." Ruthanna also had to get permission to wear a wedding gown. Captain Underwood noted again, "Approval, provided *Sounding Off*, the station newspaper, be furnished a picture show-

ing: One (1) dress, wedding, white, conventional. (Not too conventional!)"[14]

Another way the navy hoped to improve female recruitment
was to convince the prospective women and their parents that
the navy was an organization that provided appropriate housing,
religious and moral guidelines, career opportunities, and supervision. The navy emphasized that a requirement for serving in
the WAVES was an education—a college degree for officers and a
high school diploma for enlisted personnnel—and a reputation as
an individual of integrity and high moral character. It was necessary to continue to give parents information about this new career once their daughters joined the service. Parents were very
proud of their daughters in their uniforms and wanted to know
more about their daily routine.

⚓ ⚓ ⚓

By 1943, it was clear to the top navy leaders as well as the
WAVES themselves that the responsibilities of women in the navy
were changing rapidly. My first inkling that we were about to
undergo a major policy change came from an unexpected source—
First Lady Eleanor Roosevelt, who paid a surprise visit to our training school at Smith in March of 1943. When I first heard that she
was coming, I was elated that I would see her again, as I remem-
bered when, as a student at Radcliffe, I was among five students
she invited to the White House.

Eleanor Roosevelt was a very prestigious woman who had
advanced thinking about women's role in society in that she felt

Captain Herbert Underwood USN (Rtd), commanding officer of the U.S. Naval Training School at Smith College, escorts First Lady Eleanor Roosevelt on a tour of the WAVE officers' school in March 1943. Official U.S. Navy photograph.

women were equal to men—a view that was beyond what most men or women in the country were ready for. I thought of her when she was First Lady—as I think of her today—as an outstanding American woman. She did irritate a lot of male chauvinists but women who were her contemporaries thought she was wonderful. When she came to Smith College, she was not simply paying tribute to women serving in the armed forces. She also said that she hoped military women would soon receive permission to go overseas. Such legislation was pending in Congress, and she thought it would be enacted. "Overseas" in this case did not mean a foreign country, but rather meant areas under U.S. legal control which were not part of the contiguous United States—Hawaii and possibly Alaska, the West Indies, and Panama.

Other than nurses, no female naval officers or enlisted personnel went into combat areas. Had anyone suggested that they should, the idea would have been dismissed as absurd. Senior navy leaders were very proud of the WAVES and were careful about protecting them from combat areas. At that time, our nation's social values did not permit women to be in combat ships or aircraft or in war zones. I don't know how other WAVES felt, but I thought of this situation as expressing the senior officers' respect for the WAVES. In the 1990s, we have different social values than we had half a century ago. Women in the military have insisted that full equality means shared sacrifice and reward. That is the reason they felt they must serve in combat. The Defense Department has accepted this view. I welcome the changing role of women in the military, as I discuss in Chapter 8, but my evaluation of the situation in World War II is based on the attitudes and values of the 1940s—not the 1990s—and should be judged in historical perspective.

It took some time after Mrs. Roosevelt's talk at Smith before Congress provided for overseas assignments for women in the military, so my attention continued to focus on my work in the continental United States. Although I felt that my personnel work at Smith College was going well, I was still troubled because I was able to assess the civilian skills, education, and goals of the officers, but was never given the requirements of the shore jobs that the navy needed. I mentioned to Captain Underwood that the skills of the WAVE officers could be more effectively defined in our interviews if we knew what kinds of skills the navy needed in its shore establishment jobs. "I wonder if we know if the navy has something for the male reservists that tells what kinds of jobs they are going into," I said to him.

He called Captain McAfee, who in turn discussed the matter with the chief of the Bureau of Naval Personnel. He informed her that the navy did not have information on the skills or education needed for shore jobs. This lack of information was frustrating to many officers—male and female—who were assigned jobs they knew nothing about although they had skills that the navy could have used elsewhere.

The demands of war produced a change in the navy's personnel system. In August 1943, our top military leaders were under tremendous pressure to reassign experienced navy officers to the fighting forces. Many of these male officers were in shore jobs which, the navy felt, could be filled by reserve officers—male or female. In order to free regular naval officers for sea duty and at the same time make more efficient use of the skills of reservists, the navy moved to obtain the kind of information that navy personnel officers needed. To implement the new policy, the navy selected a personnel team to visit a variety of naval facilities and classify the job requirements in civilian terms. I was assigned to this team of officers. This was the second assignment I'd had since joining the WAVES. It marked an important breakthrough for women in the navy, since my input into the decision-making process affected not only navy women, but navy men as well.

In August of 1943, I left Smith for Washington, D.C., where I was assigned to the Bureau of Naval Personnel under Captain Frederick Bell, a deputy assistant officer of officer personnel. He asked me to select another woman officer to join the team, so I chose Lieutenant (jg) Ellen Miner, a delightful and competent southern woman who had personnel experience in her civilian career. In all, the team consisted of twelve officers—ten males and two females. The male officers were all reservists who had been in personnel and managerial civilian jobs, and they were respectful and considerate of their two women teammates, who were equally qualified.

Our survey took us to many places throughout the United States to observe naval facilities and activities: shipyards, air stations, navy district headquarters, supply depots, navy bureaus of ships, ordinance development offices, bureaus of aeronautics, navy yards (where ships were being built and repaired), navy real estate offices for acquisitions, graduate schools, Japanese language schools, and transportation facilities. The team worked effectively. Our surveys described, in civilian terms, the special jobs that the navy needed and the skills each job required. The kinds of jobs included administrators, managers, public relations specialists (in electronic and print media), communications specialists, code specialists, language specialists, educators, comptrollers, merchandisers (needed for procurement of uniforms and combat attire), real estate specialists (needed for acquisition and contracts of real estate), lawyers, navigation instructors, aerologists, air tower specialists, radio specialists, and engineers.

After we completed job classifications, we coded the various work experiences of the reserve officers so that their skills could be better utilized than previously. Our work marked a great improvement for the navy in making rational use of its human resources in a time of war. It also heightened the morale of *both* men and women officers in the navy reserve, as they were now given jobs—in increasing numbers—related to their civilian experience.

On October 1, 1944, I was promoted to lieutenant along with many other male and female officers. Unlike my first promotion to lieutenant (jg), the new promotion was based on the time I had spent in grade (rank) and my performance record.

⚓ ⚓ ⚓

As with so many other experiences in both my civilian and military life, external events played an enormous role in shaping my fate. When I was immersed in my work as personnel director both at Smith and Mount Holyoke, and later in Washington at the Bureau of Personnel, I certainly did not think that I would ever travel overseas. But on September 27, 1944, the law was passed permitting WAVES to volunteer for service outside the continental United States. The navy planned to place officers and enlisted WAVES in Hawaii, on three different islands—Oahu, Maui, and Hawaii.

In order to determine the kinds of jobs to which the first 500 navy women would be assigned there, someone familiar with personnel matters had to be among the first women naval officers to go to Hawaii. Captain McAfee called me and said: "I want you to leave for Hawaii in one week. Eventually, we will send a total of 5,000 navy women in the next few months." I left on October 29, flying for thirteen hours in the beautiful Pan Am Clipper aircraft from San Francisco to Oahu. The plane was so luxurious that it even had bunks for sleeping.

I was about to begin a new chapter in my life and prepare the way for the first group of WAVES to go overseas. More importantly, the arrival of 5,000 navy women overseas would denote another remarkable achievement for navy women that was bound to have lasting significance for the way the navy would perceive its female officers and enlisted personnel—not only throughout the war but in peacetime as well.

---

[1] At the time the air corps was part of the army rather than an independent service.

[2] At the beginning of U.S. participation in World War II, married men were deferred from military service—a policy that was later changed.

[3] "F" was the designation for women yeomen in World War II.

[4] With the passage of Public Law 625 in June of 1948, its name was changed to Women's Army Corps (WAC).

[5] Nylon stockings were not available during the war years.

[6] Smith College and Mount Holyoke College had been selected to become U.S. Naval Training Schools for Officers in which the WAVES would train because both were women's colleges. The navy took over some dormitories and some other offices of the colleges for the administration of the WAVES.

[7] Ruthanna Maxwell, personal interview.

[8] Ibid.

[9] Members of the choir experienced one particularly sad occasion. The staff had been invited to a dance at a nearby air base. During the evening, several of the WAVES took a ride in one of the base jeeps. The driver lost control and the car overturned. One of the girls with him was injured. Another one was killed, and a service was held in her memory. A tearful choir furnished the music.

[10] Bureau of Naval Personnel Records (WAVES).

[11] Ibid.

[12] Ensign Ruthanna Maxwell, personal report.

[13] SPARS is derived from Semper Paratus ("Always Ready").

[14] Ruthanna Maxwell, personal interview.

three

THE WAVES
GO OVERSEAS

By 1944, the women who served in the WAVES had become a component of the regular navy reserve and their lives would never be the same. Because of the contributions they were making in support of naval forces, it was beginning to be apparent—at least to the thinking of some top navy brass—that a nucleus of women should be a part of the regular and reserve navy forces. When the WAVES celebrated their second anniversary in July 1944, their numbers and work reflected their increasing importance: 10,000 in Washington and an additional 62,350 assigned throughout the United States. With this strength, the WAVES staffed ten percent of the jobs in the shore establishment and were on duty at 500 shore activities from coast to coast.[1]

As Captain McAfee's orders stated, my job was to prepare the personnel requirements for the women—officers and enlisted personnel—who would soon be sent to the three islands of Hawaii. I had only one week to pack my things and clear out of my apartment in Washington, D.C. The new assignment seemed exciting because I would be making my first trip out of the continental United States and moving into a situation that was closer to war operations. I was worried about the professional challenge of visiting naval facilities at three Hawaiian islands. I was also worried about devising detailed personnel reports for the 5,000 women officers and enlisted personnel to be sent to Hawaii. And I had severe time constraints.

As my plane was in the air en route to Hawaii, I thought of how my fellow WAVES officers and male bosses had teased me about the number of men I would be meeting in my new assignment. Pearl Harbor, as the staging area for the forward areas in the Pacific, would have a male to female ratio of about 100,000 to one. A friend of mine even jokingly drew up a design of a special "full armor" uniform for my "sea duty" in Hawaii.

When my Pan Am flight arrived at its destination in Oahu (Pearl Harbor), I was met by Captain David S. Ingalls, USNR, the commanding officer of the naval air station in Pearl Harbor. Captain Ingalls, a famous navy pilot, immediately extended an invitation for me to go to a swimming and dinner party on the Kailua side of Oahu. It was but the first of many party invitations that I was to receive and had to accept for reasons of protocol during my tour of duty in Hawaii. Parties were not on my mind, however, as I began to go to work. I was the first permanently stationed WAVE officer to go to Hawaii. In early 1944, Lieutenant Commander Jean Palmer, special assistant to the director of enlisted personnel, and Lieutenant Commander Joy Hancock, women's reserve representative, Bureau of Aeronautics, were both ordered to Hawaii to

Lieutenant Quick is welcomed to Pearl Harbor, November 1, 1944. Official U.S. Navy photograph.

THE SECRETARY OF THE NAVY AND MRS. FORRESTAL

REQUEST THE PLEASURE OF THE COMPANY OF

Lieutenant Quick

ON *August 1st, 1944*

AT *1642 - 29th St.* at *8* O'CLOCK

Buffet dinner in honor of Ranking Women Officers of the Navy

R. S. V. P.

A typical invitation to one of the many social events Lieutenant Quick was obligated to attend while in Hawaii.

review housing plans, living conditions, and location assignments for the WAVES who would be going there. When Captain McAfee resigned from the navy soon afterward to return to her duties as president of Wellesley College, Jean Palmer was promoted to commander to serve as interim director. Joy Hancock was promoted to captain and assumed her duties as director of the WAVES on July 26, 1944. Hancock reported to the Bureau of Naval Personnel on February 26, 1946, as assistant director of plans. On July 26, 1946, Hancock became director of the U.S. Women's Naval Reserve with the rank of captain.

In December 1944, Lieutenant Commander Eleanor Rigby, director of women who served in the fourteenth naval district, and Lieutenant Marion Sheldon, specialist for aviation activities, arrived on the islands. First Class Yeomen Mary Iacino and Geraldine McGee also arrived that month, with assignments to assist me in my duties as the district personnel officer. Like me, my two yeoman assistants were thrilled and delighted to be in Pearl Harbor. Since the navy women's housing facilities were under construction, however, there was no place for them to stay except in a hospital dispensary, which had no recreational facilities and no mess—only sleeping quarters. Once the women got to their housing facilities, there was no transportation they could use to go to recreational activities. The month of December proved to be a difficult time because they were the only female naval personnel (with the exception of navy nurses), the men had seen. They were looked at with the same bewilderment as if two Martians had just dropped in from outer space. As enlisted personnel, they had to eat in the general mess where all of the enlisted men had their meals. Every time they walked in, hundreds of men would stand, applaud, and whistle.

Iacino and McGee were two wonderful young women who adjusted well to the strange new world. Traditionally in the navy, there was supposed to be a social distance between officers and enlisted personnel. I never had that feeling of social distance generally, and I certainly did not feel it with these two women. I was "boss," but I did not need to emphasize my status. We became very close friends. Usually on the weekends, I would take them to dinner and to island locations in my jeep. We had some very happy times together.

When they first arrived, however, I had just one month to determine what jobs and skills the WAVES needed in Hawaii. I had

Lieutenant Quick welcomes her two first class yeomen arriving at Pearl Harbor, December 1944. (l–r) Lieutenant Quick, First Class Yeoman Mary Iacino and First Class Yeoman Geraldine Magee. Official U.S. Navy photograph.

to fly to three different islands and map out my report, assessing the personnel requirements for each of the stations I went to. Based on my report, Yeomen Iacino and McGee compiled the data that the different navy commands on each island requested. We had to have all of our work completed by the time the first group of 500 women (from what was anticipated as an eventual total of 5,000) would be arriving in early January 1945. We met our deadline, although we all worked long hours. The jobs described in the report were similar to the jobs navy women already held within the continental United States. In all, there were thirty identifiable jobs for enlisted women, including control tower operators, storekeepers, hospital corpsmen, aviation machinist mates, electricians mates, radio technicians, and parachute riggers. In some instances, the women would replace men who would then go to the forward areas, but for the most part they would be stepping into jobs created by the growing demands of war.

By the time the first group of 500 WAVES arrived, the navy construction crew (Seabees) had done a magnificent job in converting Quonset huts which had been occupied by enlisted men into housing facilities for the WAVES. They added cubicles with two bunks, and cement floors with an attractive synthetic covering. The interior of each Quonset was painted in a pastel shade, an appealing way the Seabees thought of to welcome the enlisted women. Each Quonset accommodated thirty-two women. In addition, the occupants of every three Quonset huts had shower and toilet facilities as well as hair dryers and laundry facilities. One of every eight huts was a recreation facility. An additional large recreation area included an open-air movie theatre, playing fields, tennis courts, dance floor, ship service store, chapel, and a medical dispensary. Women officers, including me, were assigned to live in the bachelor officers' quarters at the naval air base in Honolulu, which were being converted to house women officers who were coming to the Pearl Harbor area. The housing facilities of Maui and Hawaii had similar excellent accommodations for women, both officers and enlisted personnel.

In early January 1945, the first 500 WAVES marched down the gang plank, much to the delight of the press and the male military personnel in the vicinity. All of these women—as well as the others who came to Hawaii later—had specifically volunteered and were approved for overseas duty.

The women officers were surprised to find that some of the navy men at the Pearl Harbor naval station had built a two-foot high "wolf fence" around their quarters to "protect" them from predatory male animals who might be roaming in the neighborhood. The WAVE officers as well as the male officers were amused by this joke.

The housing situation improved for senior WAVE officers within a few months of my arrival. Early in 1945, Admiral Chester Nimitz, fleet commander for the Pacific, moved his command to Guam. Consequently, one of the admiral's staff—Admiral John Perry, chief of the navy's famed construction engineers—vacated his eight Quonset huts. Admiral Jack Towers, who was then the senior officer in Pearl Harbor, asked me if I would like them. After inspecting them, I readily said "Yes." They were luxurious compared to the bachelor officers' quarters. Each hut had two bedrooms, two baths, a living room between the bedrooms, a large

The "wolf fence" erected to "protect" women officers at their proposed quarters, Naval Air Station, Honolulu, Hawaii, December 1944. Official U.S. Navy photograph.

kitchen, and an attractive lounge. The new facilities provided housing for thirty-two of the senior women officers.

I was assigned a chief navy cook and two navy stewards. The cook had spent thirty years in the navy, and this was the first time that his boss was a woman. I was not sure how to handle a chief, especially since I could tell that he was very unhappy. Moreover, he was not a very good cook. Our first controversy came when he cooked frozen vegetables for one hour, and I suggested that just a few minutes was enough time. We spent some time in the galley, and he had to endure my suggestions for disposing of leftovers and maintaining cleanliness. I could see that he didn't think too highly of his new boss.

The two stewards were young Filipinos who had been successful in fighting the Japanese in their country. My rapport with them was about the same as it was with the chief. I also had difficulty communicating with them because they spoke little English. I decided to do something to establish a better rapport with all three men. Upon inspecting their quarters, I found them very bare, so I obtained some radios, drapes, lounging chairs, desks, and pictures for the walls. Our rapport improved dramatically. My weekly inspections resulted in superior cleanliness and liberty (time off).

⚓ ⚓ ⚓

Being a woman naval officer in Pearl Harbor among many thousands of foreign service, navy, army, and marine men was a unique experience. Very few of the military men had ever seen a navy woman officer, so the greetings, whistles, and applause were continuous. At each command I visited, there were special social activities for the evenings after exceedingly busy work days. Fortunately, I "survived" these long and exciting days.

As is often the case in social gatherings among people working in the same organization, comments are made that offer insights about colleagues' attitudes toward work matters. On one occasion, for example, I was invited to a dinner party at the Destroyer Officers Club. My dinner partner was Vice Admiral Charles Lockwood, who, I learned later, was commander of the Submarine Forces, Pacific. I said to him: "Are you getting any WAVES at your command, sir?"

"Dear God, no," he replied. "I have enough trouble handling the Japanese."

I guess he felt sorry later that he had been so abrupt, because his aide called a few days later and extended an invitation on behalf of Admiral Lockwood to meet the commanding officer of a successful submarine patrol that had sunk many Japanese ships, Commander A. Gene Fluckey, who took command of the U.S.S. *Barb* early in 1944.[2] I was honored to meet such an illustrious and brave officer. We had lunch on board the submarine *Barb* in the commanding officer's quarters. Commander Fluckey related many stories of his perilous and successful encounters with Japanese ships, which he later described in *Thunder Below!*[3] Commander Fluckey was awarded four Navy Crosses and the Congressional Medal of Honor for his service in World War II.

Another exciting social occasion included a luncheon at the quarters of Fleet Admiral Nimitz, whose aide had called to say that the admiral would like to invite me to lunch. I replied that I would have to speak with my boss and then call back. Since I had been in the navy only two years, I was nervous at the prospect of having lunch with Admiral Nimitz, who commanded U.S. and allied ships and aircraft and hundreds of thousands of troops in the vast Pacific war zone. As a mere lieutenant, I was a bundle of nerves at the prospect of meeting him.

"Are you sure Admiral Nimitz invited you to lunch?" my boss asked me.

"This is his aide's name and number," I said. "I told him that after I talked with you, I would call him back. Do I have to accept?"

"That's his aide all right," he said. "Anything that Admiral Nimitz wants you to do in Pearl Harbor, we do. I'll get you a sedan and a marine driver so you can go in style."

I had met a few admirals before but had never been in a social situation with an officer of such high rank. I was nervous about the protocol, as my training classes back at Smith provided me with no guide for this particular type of encounter. I kept thinking: I'm a woman but I'm also a naval officer, so how should I handle this? When I arrived I saw the admiral and his aide standing above the stairs up on the lanai (porch). I had for some reason assumed I was to have lunch only with Admiral Nimitz and his aide, but when I walked into the dining room, I was surprised to see that it was filled with officers. I had never seen so many captains and admirals in my life—all male. Admiral Nimitz had invited his entire operations staff.

When I left, I was not sure what we had discussed during the luncheon. At the time, I thought that I had done very well conversationally and acted properly. But a week later, when I encountered Admiral Nimitz at a reception, I began having second thoughts about my performance when he said, "You have become a very famous lieutenant. My staff has reviewed navy history. You are the first lieutenant in the history of the navy to blow a kiss to a fleet admiral instead of saluting and not be court-martialed. I knew things would change now that the WAVES are here, and I must admit that I kind of like it."

In my excitement at meeting Admiral Nimitz at the luncheon, I had no idea that I made such a faux pas!

Reception for Fleet Admiral Chester Nimitz, Navy Day, Pearl Harbor, October 1945. Official U.S. Navy photograph.

Although I did not know it at the time, the luncheon was to be a particularly important event in my life for personal reasons. At the end of it, after I thanked Admiral Nimitz for inviting me, Captain Howard Collins asked if he could escort me down the steps. We spoke for a few moments as we walked to my car, and I saw him again at a reception shortly thereafter. Within a few weeks, however, he went on sea duty as the commander of a destroyer and I did not meet him again until after the war was over.

Although my work took up most of my time in Hawaii, I very much enjoyed the opportunities to attend luncheons and parties and participate in recreational activities in such a magnificent setting. A Denver millionaire offered the navy women officers a beautiful home on the Kailua side of Oahu for recreational use, and he included the services of a maid and a male steward to take care of household chores. After the navy approved the offer, I went with two of my fellow officers—Winifred Love and Louise Wilde, classmates from my days at Smith—to investigate the home and to go swimming on a Saturday afternoon. I was the first one dressed after swimming. We were happy to be out of uniform, and I was wearing an aloha shirt and shorts. As I went into the living room, I saw a man approaching our front door, and he, too, was wearing an aloha shirt and shorts. I opened the door and said: "Would you care to come in?"

"I certainly would," he replied. "I've been walking up and down the beach and am feeling very warm. I hope I might have a peek at this beautiful home."

Although the visitor did not give his name, I recognized him. His picture was often on the front pages of newspapers and the covers of magazines. He came in and sat down. When I introduced myself as Winifred Quick, he still did not mention his name. I asked him if he would like to have a drink, and when I got a positive response I sent the steward for it. He returned in a few minutes, very meticulously dressed in his white coat, about the same time my two friends came into the living room.

"These are my friends, Winifred Love and Louise Wilde," I said to our guest, who quite suddenly looked at his watch and said: "I must leave, as I'm late for an appointment." We were rather surprised and wondered if we had done something wrong as we watched him hurrying down the beach, but we dismissed any further speculation.

The next morning, the phone rang at about nine o'clock. I answered, saying, "Lieutenant Quick speaking."

"This is Admiral Carney, chief of staff to Admiral Halsey.[4] Did you know who your guest was yesterday?"

"Yes, sir," I said.

"Had you ever met him?"

"No, sir."

"Why didn't you tell him that you were in the navy?"

"He didn't tell me that he was in the navy."

"Well, I must tell you what happened when Admiral Halsey came back to our recreational center," Admiral Carney said. "Admiral Halsey told us it was providential that he went into that house. 'It was only an eighth of a mile distant from ours, and three very attractive women live there,' he said. 'You won't believe their names—Quick, Wilde, Love. I'm positive they are spies. They live in a very luxurious home with a 125-foot living room— beautifully furnished. I can anticipate them putting on their pretty little bathing suits and tripping down an eighth of a mile to where our officers recreation quarters are, getting acquainted with our staff officers, and finding out our forward plans.'"

By this time of the conversation, I didn't know what to think. Admiral Carney continued: "Admiral Halsey then asked his aide to find out from Intelligence all the information available about those three women—who owns the house, and everything about it. 'Tell them this is urgent,' he said, 'and I want it by eight o'clock tomorrow morning.' At eight o'clock, the aide came in. 'Well, what's the story?' the admiral asked. 'A Denver millionaire gave it to the naval officers for the duration,' the aide said. 'I didn't see any naval officers there,' returned the admiral. 'Oh, I'm sorry, sir, *women* naval officers,' said the aide. 'Oh, dear God,' said Admiral Halsey. 'Even the Japanese didn't do this to me.'"

I had all I could do to restrain my laughter. I managed to retain my composure long enough to hear Admiral Carney's concluding comment: "On behalf of Admiral Halsey, myself, and the officers of the Third Fleet, we would like to invite the three spies to brunch and a swimming party. We will send a car at eleven. Bring your bathing suits."

I appreciated the excitement at being invited to the social gatherings of such august people as Admirals Nimitz and Halsey and the staff officers who had just returned from a critical and hazardous battle with the Japanese. I was aware of the many kindnesses and attention that my fellow officers gave in arranging for housing and recreation, and I liked the gracious manners of the male officers during working and social occasions. On one occasion when I had flown to Washington with Admiral Towers in his special plane, Commander George Anderson, a navy aviator on Admiral Towers's staff, had taken my khaki-colored army jeep and had it painted light blue with white fringe on top—definitely not navy issue. He thought that I shouldn't be driving a vehicle that looked like a man's jeep. I was thrilled to have such a unique jeep, the only one of its kind in Hawaii. George Anderson was a most competent and charming officer as well as being one of the most handsome men I had ever seen. He later became chief of naval operations.

⚓ ⚓ ⚓

Unlike most male military personnel, I gave no consideration to what I would do when the war was over. In fact, in 1944, I thought that the war would go on for years. When the United States dropped the atomic bomb on Hiroshima in August 1945, I was like most Americans—unaware of such a weapon. Even after I heard the news about the second atomic bomb being dropped at Nagasaki, I could not imagine it. My notion of "big weapons" at the time were the bombers and their powerful conventional bomb payloads.

When President Harry S Truman announced that Japan had accepted defeat, Pearl Harbor became the scene of a huge fireworks display. Every ship was lit up; simulated bombs and firecrackers went off; all of Hawaii was jubilant. I felt great relief that no more of our American boys would be killed in World War II and that I would not have to watch from my office window when the ships of war loaded with sailors and marines sailed away. Now that the war was over, I would not have to wonder how many of these young men would come back alive.

When World War II came to an end, women had established a remarkable legacy of *woman*power in the U.S. military. The navy in 1942 originally visualized the maximum strength of the naval women reserve at approximately 11,000, and plans were formulated with that number in mind. It soon became evident that this thinking was not sufficiently imaginative. Shortly before Japan was defeated, there were approximately 86,000 women in the navy and 19,000 women in the marines, stationed at some 950 shore activities in the United States and Hawaii and serving in practically all ratings except those from which they were excluded because of physical limitations, combatant nature, or sea-going requirements. Women could no longer be looked upon as merely "replacements." The war years proved that the work they had done contributed much to the overall efficiency of the service. Particularly in the fields of communication, clerical work, hospital work, navy aviation, and supply, women demonstrated their usefulness, patience, and thoroughness by performing many duties equal to or better than men had done.

Still, women did not have total acceptance in the navy. Although most of the senior male officers were very supportive of the WAVES, many navy personnel—both officer and enlisted—were not as enthusiastic, and some were even hostile. Many U.S. Navy men—like many other American men—still had highly developed sexist ideas about women which had been generated by their cultural background. Moreover, many navy men had never worked side by side with women before and now had to adapt to what would be described today as culture shock. Some of this opposition possibly arose out of fear generated by the fact that the navy women had better educations than most of the enlisted navy men. Also, some enlisted men reasoned that they might not advance as fast as they hoped because the women might be better qualified in the testing program.[5]

I rarely encountered this hostility with male officers, but an exception occurred when I was reassigned to a policy job in the Bureau of Naval Personnel after World War II. Specifically, my problems arose when I tried to establish rotation policies for women officers in a manner allowing them to have career patterns similar to those of male officers at equal levels of responsibility, assignments, examinations, and promotion. Apparently, some of the male navy officers resisted such an innovation because they still looked at women navy officers as civilians in the civil service. It was not unusual for me to find that, on an individual basis, a male officer might recognize the professional competence of a particular WAVE associate, but be unable to generalize from his experience in order to regard any other woman in the WAVES as a professional.

The effect of some negative attitudes about women in the navy put great strains on individual navy women. Each WAVE—officer or enlisted—had to go through a continual process of proving herself to her male associates in every new situation. It was usually the case that once a commanding officer had WAVES assigned to his command, he became impressed with their education and proficiency and would then request additional WAVES.

After Japan was defeated, nobody knew for certain what to make of this legacy of women in the navy. Americans wanted to return to normal peacetime conditions, like they had done after World War I. The nation was about to demobilize—to reduce the huge numbers of armed forces personnel and to lower its military spending. Nobody was sure in August 1945 whether demobilization might mean phasing out women from the armed services entirely.

Personally, I had little time to think of such weighty matters. While most navy women in Hawaii gave immediate thought to returning home and getting on with their lives, I did not have that option. Just about the time I was beginning to think about returning to Pasadena and looking for a civilian job, Admiral S. A.

Taffinger, commandant of the Fourteenth Naval District, asked me to remain to develop plans for the demobilization, transportation, and release from the navy of over 4,400 WAVES in the Hawaiian islands.

---

[1] Bureau of Naval Personnel Records (WAVES).

[2] The year 1944 was the golden year for our submarines in World War II, as American underwater raiders sank nearly twice as many enemy ships as they had done the year before.

[3] University of Illinois Press, 1992.

[4] Admiral Mick Carney and Admiral Bill Halsey, the latter being commander, U.S. Third Fleet.

[5] Enlisted men and women took the same qualifying examinations. Promotion was based on the results of tests.

four

WOMEN IN THE
POST-WORLD WAR II
NAVY: 1945–1957

Had the United States returned to a policy of isolationism after World War II like it did after World War I, quite possibly there would have been no women in the navy after 1945. But international developments made women's permanent involvement in the postwar U.S. Navy a necessity. The emergence of the Cold War, with its constant distrust, rivalry, diplomatic maneuvering, and military buildups between the two superpowers, meant that the United States had to be continuously prepared to meet any challenge by the Soviet Union and other communist countries. Moreover, changing military technology—principally the birth of the atomic age and the development of long-range delivery systems—made the United States more vulnerable to overseas military initiatives than it had ever been before.

Top military leaders recognized that women played an important role in World War II and that they were bound to play an equally important role in any future wars. They reasoned that it would be counterproductive and time-consuming to go through all the start-up efforts to activate women into the armed services again in a new emergency, so most military leaders agreed that there should continue to be a nucleus of women both in the regular and the reserve services.

Although high-level military officials were enthusiastic supporters of bringing women into the postwar military, I don't think that they—or anyone else—fully understood at the time the difficulties of implementing the policy. Once that nucleus was established, the status of women in the armed forces evolved to a point at which women achieved higher ranks, a broader range of assignments, and greater recognition than many males in the military had ever imagined—or ever wanted. Every gain for women in the military was achieved only after a long battle with ignorance, military tradition, entrenched interests, male chauvinism, or some combination of these tough barriers. And the battle started within a few months after Japan had been defeated, mostly because many civilians and politicians held negative attitudes about the need for military women in peacetime.

⚓ ⚓ ⚓

At war's end, I was not thinking of foreign or national policy issues, but was preoccupied with getting women military personnel back home quickly from overseas assignments. "Bringing the boys back home" (and the girls, too) was easier said than done. Millions of soldiers and sailors were stationed overseas, and the principal method of getting them home was by ship, with only a small number returning by air transport. All the men and women in the Pacific came through Pearl Harbor. How quickly they left Hawaii depended on their priority rating and length of service. Those who had been in the navy the longest were the first to go home.

The first navy women to leave Pearl Harbor did so in October of 1945. As district personnel officer for navy women at Pearl Harbor and the two other islands at that time, I was asked to set up all the plans for demobilizing the WAVES there. Admiral S. A. Taffinger recommended that I be spot-promoted to lieutenant commander, and this promotion was instantly approved. My two yeomen (whom I had helped get promoted to chief—a big boost for them) also agreed to stay on to help me.[1]

The demobilization plan required a personnel officer to conduct an exit interview with each individual and to bring her records up to date. Departing navy personnel had to take a physical examination in which any disabilities were recorded so that disability pay could be approved.

When the war ended, most WAVES were not considering staying in the service, but were instead anxious to return to civilian life. My own yearning was not as desperate as that of many other navy women, however, because I had at least been able to make several trips to Washington for consultations about personnel matters. I had even been able to attend my brother Larry's graduation at the U.S. Naval Academy in 1945, because it coincided with one of my trips.

During demobilization, the navy realized that some reserve personnel would need to be retained on active duty. These individuals had to send via their commanding officers to the Bureau of Personnel a request for retention. If approved, most of the officers and enlisted personnel received a temporary promotion to the next higher rank or rating. Approximately 450 women officers and 16,000 enlisted women remained on active duty. The rest of the 8,000 WAVE officers and 70,000 enlisted women were demobilized along with the millions of male reservists.[2]

When my demobilization duties were finished, I returned to Washington, D.C., in August 1946, and was given a temporary assignment with the Potomac River Naval Command at the navy yard. By this time, I was not sure whether or not I wanted to stay in the service. Assistant Chief for Naval Personnel Joy Hancock told me that the navy was considering plans to have a core of women in the regular and reserve navy and that she was in charge of settling questions on personnel matters before the legislation could be proposed. She asked me: "Would you stay in the navy and work on this?"

This was a job that nobody had ever done before, and it seemed to promise a mental challenge, which is the kind of job I like. It never occurred to me that I might be missing out on a terrific job in civilian life, because I had already had two very good civilian job experiences. In the fall of 1946, I began working in the Bureau of Personnel in the Officer Division. I was put in charge of developing standards for women officers that would cover requirements for age, education, performance, and physical condition for possible acceptance in the regular navy. I also devised plans for the effective utilization of a nucleus of women in the active naval forces. I consulted with the senior officers responsible for each area of policy for which a change was proposed. I tried to apply guidelines for women that were similar to those already established for men (except for sea duty), but it was not always possible. It was impractical, for instance, to apply the same age requirements for women in transferring to the regular navy. We wanted women who had navy reserve experience to become part of the regular navy, but these women were older than their male counterparts, the latter of whom were appointed as ensigns from college or the Naval Academy. For women, we established a "grandfather clause" which permitted them to transfer to the regular navy as ensigns, lieutenant (jgs), lieutenants, lieutenant commanders, and commanders, at age levels higher than their male counterparts.

Getting approval for our guidelines was slow. We were dealing with a radical new concept—women in the peacetime regular navy, so even more deliberation was required than usually took place in a bureaucratic process. When I met with opposition, I tried to figure out a professional way to make my case in a reasonable manner. I would say, for example, "Well, captain (or admiral), I really hoped I would get your help on this because it is a new situation for me and I am trying to put it in a proper navy policy framework similar to what was done for the male officers. I need your help and guidance on these proposed policies."

And he would sometimes say: "Well, I don't see any reason for women to be in the navy."

"I'm sorry, sir," I would reply. "I've been told that the navy is going to propose the enactment of legislation that women be made part of the reserve and regular navy. I've been asked to prepare the navy guidelines for the appointment and transfer of these women. If you object to anything I've written, please give me your suggestions so that I can make corrections." These papers had to be reviewed by many officers. If an officer approved, he initialed the report. If not, he wrote his recommendations on the back so that the chief of naval personnel could see his objection. He would do that with great hesitancy, however, because if the chief of naval personnel favored a policy, the resisting officer would need to have strong and defensible objections.

It was 1947 before the Senate Armed Services Committee finally conducted hearings about allowing women to become members of the regular and reserve services. The House Armed Services Committee considered the same subject in 1948. I attended or followed a number of the hearings since I had done so much work on the subject, and was delighted when navy leaders and members of Congress spoke well about the contributions that the WAVES had made to the navy. But the legislators had some strange ideas about women, which were based on attitudes that we can only describe today as sexist. Some of these ideas became the rationale for Congress to limit opportunities for women in the navy, creating unnecessarily burdensome restrictions. First, Congress limited the number of women allowed to join to two percent of the total regular navy. Second, it sought to have enlisted women assigned to specialized designation in yeoman, hospital, corpsman, aviation mechanic, and other categories in which there was a much larger percentage of shore billets for that rate than sea duties. In this way, there would be no interference with navy enlisted men's rotation between sea duty and shore duty.[3] Third, Congress was careful to exclude women from the higher ranks of the navy. Captain was the highest rank a woman could attain, and only one woman at a time could hold that temporary rank in the entire navy. Immediately below her was the rank of commander, and Congress also placed a strict limit on the numbers of women commanders.

As rationale for their decisions, the Senate Armed Services Committee members reasoned that women showed signs of aging faster than men did. Despite all the statistical evidence we provided, the committee members retained their sexually-biased views about women. As a result, women in the service had to live with the legislative consequences of this prejudice for many years. Congress provided that a woman lieutenant commander who reached the age of fifty and had not held commander rank had to retire. Period. Even if a woman navy officer reached the rank of commander, she had to retire at the age of fifty-five. I listened in amazement to congressional discussions about women, and in particular about menopause. These men thought that menopause would preclude women's participation in the regular navy. Senator Leverett Saltonstall of Massachusetts commented:

On the assumption that some women become physically and emotionally below par during the menopause period, and that a regular corps will contain more in this age group than was the case in the wartime group, what is to be the policy in handling such cases? Is there any parallel in civil life? Will they be retired as "physically incapacitated"? Can they be separated from the service without paying them some form of severance pay, thereby increasing the relative cost of the program over that of male personnel?[4]

The committee men who asked such questions were well past fifty-five years in age themselves, and they were obviously unafraid that advanced age impeded the effectiveness of their work. Vice Admiral Thomas Sprague, chief of naval personnel, assured Senator Saltonstall that in the previous five years, none of the eighteen WAVE retirements was related to menopause or any other female "disease." He said, "Approximately sixteen percent of the 500 WAVE officers presently on duty are over forty years of age. The navy medical statistics do not indicate that women become less fit for active duty beyond the age of forty."[5]

To furnish scientific opinion, the navy sought and received a written statement from the surgeon general of the navy, Rear Admiral Clifford A. Swanson, who confirmed the view that there is no difference between men and women as far as retirement from the navy for reasons of physical disability was concerned. He added: "The commonly held idea that many women are invalidated in their middle years by the onset of the menopause is largely a popular fallacy. It is well known that men pass through the same physiological change resembling that in women."[6] Congressmen were embarrassed when they learned of the surgeon general's letter because they had been unaware that men—including those on the committee—went through male menopause. And that was the end of the discussion on the subject.

What was interesting about the congressional hearings was that some matters which had once been big issues received little or no attention. For example, there was no challenge to allowing navy women to serve abroad. Navy women had served as flight orderlies in air transport squadrons as early as World War II, but at that time their duty was limited to the continental United States. In 1948, they were permitted to take assignments in Europe and elsewhere. But certain restrictions continued. Women were not allowed to serve on aircraft or ships designated for combat.[7] The idea that women could serve in combat was not even considered since there was no support for such a change in the navy, Congress, or public opinion.

The House hearings raised the issue of racial minority participation in jobs for navy women. Leslie S. Perry, legislative representative of the National Association for the Advancement of Colored People, urged a provision that would ban discrimination and segregation in the proposed legislation. Perry said that until October 1944, the navy had not accepted female minority applicants, and changing its policy at that point brought in only a token number of applicants. (The army and the marines had similar exclusionary experiences.) In 1945, only two out of 8,000 women navy officers were classified as "Negro" (the descriptive term used for African Americans in the 1940s and 1950s); and only seventy out of 78,000 enlisted women were classified as such. By the time of the House hearings in 1948, there was not a single black officer in the WAVES out of a total of 430 officers, and there were only six black enlisted women out of 1,700.[8]

It is sad that while women as a group were fighting for inclusion into the navy and were making grudging—but significant—gains, African-American women were not benefiting from those gains. At that time, few African-American or other minority women even applied to the navy or other services, in large part because of the considerable prejudice against African Americans held by the various services, as well as civilian society. On July 26, 1948, President Truman issued Executive Order 9981, which required equivalent treatment and opportunity for all military personnel. This was the order that desegregated the armed forces and led eventually to increased participation by racial minorities in the military.

Public Law 625, the Women's Armed Forces Integration Act, was signed by President Truman on June 12, 1948. Eight enlisted WAVES were sworn into the regular navy at that time. Rear Admiral George Russell, judge advocate general of the navy, gave the oath, with Secretary of the Navy John Sullivan and Captain Hancock witnessing the ceremony. The enlisted women were Kay Langdon, Wilma Marcel, Wilma Ballenger, Edna Young, Edna Shannon, Doris Robertson, Doris Johnson, and Frances Devany. On October 15 of that year, the first eight of the 288 officers selected for the regular navy were sworn in by Rear Admiral Russell, with Secretary of the Navy Sullivan again witnessing the ceremony. These eight were: Captain Joy Bright Hancock, Lieutenant Commander Winifred Redden Quick, Lieutenant Ann King, Lieutenant Frances Willoughby, Lieutenant Ellen Ford, Lieutenant Doris

Cranmore, Lieutenant (jg) Doris Defenderfer, and Lieutenant (jg) Betty Tennant. The eight officers came from different specialties of the navy, as did the eight enlisted women.

⚓ ⚓ ⚓

Although the legislation making women a part of the regular navy necessitated a change in some administrative policies, other practices were retained to maintain continuity in the system. Since 1942, for example, the director of the WAVES had formulated guidelines regarding policies for the administration of the women's naval reserve. At each major command, a woman officer was appointed as Assistant (W),[9] and at smaller commands, the commanding officer appointed a female officer as Women's Representative (WR). A woman holding either of these assignments advised the senior officer on matters concerning the administration of navy women. When women became a part of the regular and reserve navy, these guidelines were gradually incorporated into navy regulations.

I stayed on as assigment and women's policy officer at the Bureau of Personnel and worked to help the navy implement the new legislation. I was responsible for developing career ladders and promotion, rotation, and other policies, and for compiling reports for my superiors. When designing a career ladder for women which would give them greater responsibility as they progressed in rank, I patterned the policies as closely as I could on those in effect for male officers. One problem I dealt with was that during World War II a large number of navy women had been relegated to communications work even though they were capable of more specialized assignments. I transferred these officers to more suitable assignments as quickly as I could. This task was made easier because I was also the assignment and policy officer, assigning women officers to different billets and more responsible jobs as they progressed in rank. I extracted information on some of those women who had been in communications for a number of years, reviewed their backgrounds, and found assignments with increased responsibility in the naval shore activities in which they could contribute far more than they had been able to as communicators.

I initiated a rotation policy for women officers similar to that of navy men. Under the policy the women officers were reassigned every two to three years to a different and more responsible job than the previous one. The purpose of this rotation policy was for the officers to acquire increasing and more diversified skills and experiences as they rose in rank. I felt it was necessary for women officers to have a similar rotation policy in order to reap the same benefits as their male counterparts.

Some senior officers opposed the rotation policy for women. One of the statements I used to argue with them was: "Congress passed a law to permit women to be a part of the regular navy. The chief of the bureau knows that we must have a sound plan for utilizing these women officers. I have been assigned the task of developing a policy through which the navy will utilize and train women so that they will be placed in assignments with responsibilities commensurate with their ranks. A rotation plan will give women officers a variety of assignments—from ensign to commander—so they will be able to contribute to the navy the same as their male counterparts."

In addition to plans for rotation and job opportunities, a promotion plan for each rank had to be developed so that women could compete for promotion to a higher rank based on their navy achievements. With such a promotion plan, the navy—through selection boards—would be able to compare the quality of work of either male or female officers of the same rank. These boards needed to take into consideration the fact that since women officers were restricted from sea duty, the kinds of jobs and the responsibilities they held would be different from the men's. The women would be evaluated by their commanding officers in the fitness report for each officer. All navy officers—men and women—would be periodically evaluated on their performance in each assignment.

A big problem, however, was that some of the navy men had not accepted the fact that women could be as competent as men. For the most part, this was a result of the fact that most of the men in senior ranks had never worked with civilian women or women officers, and they found this a complex adjustment. Fortunately, most of my proposed policies regarding rotation and other personnel policies for women during this period were eventually approved. I used tact and diplomacy, and I also did my homework very, very carefully in order to answer the objections I anticipated the senior male officers would bring up. It was an interesting and challenging job, as I was constantly confronted with negative attitudes about navy women, even though most senior officers were cordial and helpful.

Because the navy needed a policy for women in every area it had a policy for men, I often began by presenting my recommendations to ten different captains—each of whom was responsible for a specific policy area. These consultations were immensely important and helpful to me. Each senior male officer needed to approve each proposed new policy for women, after which I would have to get the approval of his boss—an admiral in the Officer Division of the Bureau of Personnel. At that point I would have to go through the Planning and Policy Division, where the proposed policies often underwent more revision. Finally, Captain Hancock and the chief of the bureau, a senior admiral, needed to give approval. In spite of the negotiating difficulties I faced, new policies *were* devised, although it took months for each new proposal to get approved. Women—officer and enlisted—made many gradual advances before I left my assignment in the Bureau of Naval Personnel in August 1950.

In late 1950, college women were authorized, along with college men, to become officer candidates. The program provided for two six-week periods of training during summer vacations while in college and also after graduation. Upon completion of training, if the candidates had reached the age of twenty-one, they (both men and women) were commissioned ensigns in the reserve and were ordered to active duty. The first course for women, at Great Lakes Training Center outside of Chicago, was coeducational. Later it was moved to the Recruit (W) School at Bainbridge, Maryland, and then to the U.S. Naval Indoctrination School for Officers (W) in Newport, Rhode Island. Navy men also attended the Newport school, but the women studied separately because they were taking courses in nonseagoing specialties different from those taken by the men.

The number of women in the navy was influenced by both budgetary constraints and military requirements. At the time of the passage of Public Law 625 in 1948, there were 416 navy women officers (288 regular and 128 reserves) and 1,510 enlisted women (regular and reserve). By the time of the Korean War in 1952, the need for increased personnel resulted in both men and women reservists being called to active duty, resulting in approximately 8,500 enlisted women and 1,000 women officers, in the active reserve and regular navy forces.

Navy women continued to be given new responsibilities. In August of 1953, navy women in the Hospital Corps were assigned to hospital ships and to Military Sea Transport Service ships. By 1957, enlisted women were eligible to hold twenty-five of the navy's sixty-two General Service (GS) ratings. The ratings excluded for enlisted women consisted of those requiring considerable physical strength and those that were primarily seagoing. From 1957 on, as chief of naval personnel for women, I made continuous efforts to expand both job and educational opportunities for navy women. (See Chapter 5.) By 1962, women officers served in the medical corps, medical service corps (administrative and pharmaceutical), dental corps, supply corps, and civil engineer corps. Women officers in air activities served as aerologists, air transport officers, naval air navigators and link celestial navigation instructors. These were the first women officers to perform duties as part of a military air crew. They wore the wings of the naval air navigators and made flights within the continental United States and overseas. Also by 1962 when I retired from the navy, women personnel were serving in Puerto Rico, Alaska, the Philippines, Guam, Hawaii, Japan, Great Britain, France, Italy, Norway, and West Germany. (See Chapter 6.)

⚓ ⚓ ⚓

When I left the Bureau of Personnel in 1950, I was assigned to the office of the secretary of defense. My job was to assist in developing a comprehensive plan for military personnel assigned to that office. This was a new job for a woman officer. Two unique aspects of the job were (1) that I was responsible for more than one service, and (2) that I was dealing with assignments for both men and women—although mostly men. For the first time in my military career, I had a personnel job, not a *female personnel* job. In addition, I was the only woman officer assigned to the secretary of defense staff at the time.

The assignment was difficult because there were areas of conflict between civilian and military personnel within the office. Most of the staff were high-echelon civilians, since at that time some professional military officers were reluctant to serve there. They felt the work had no relation to their service career pattern. They saw an assignment there as a kiss of death, professionally speaking.

My assignment was to survey military positions needed in the office so that the director of civilian personnel would be able to distinguish between the jobs that should go to the professional military officers and those that should go to civilians. To accomplish this goal, it was necessary to understand which jobs required military experience rather than civilian expertise. Each job classification defined the qualification requirements and determined the appropriate experience for each position—military or civilian—so that the qualified officer or civilian could be selected. The real problem, from the individual officer's standpoint, was that the officers did not get the same credit for serving in the office of the secretary of defense as they would on a regular career pattern in their service.

This survey was a pioneering effort without precedent or guidelines. It was important to the military officers—army, navy, marines, and air force—that they receive comparable service credit to assure them the opportunity of promotion with their peers. My work facilitated the development of a plan to make assignments to the office of the secretary of defense more career-enhancing. My report was approved by a senior military officer in the Department of Defense; my fitness report was highly favorable for this assignment and I was strongly recommended for promotion.

⚓ ⚓ ⚓

Because my previous job had dealt with so many controversial personnel and professional matters, I welcomed my next assignment, as I was selected for graduate work at Stanford University. The navy had a program allowing navy officers to spend a year of graduate study there, and I had applied for the program even before I joined the office of the secretary of defense. A selection board chose me—along with fourteen men and women navy and marine officers—for the year's graduate work. The program at Stanford allowed the selected navy officers to take any courses they wanted in different graduate programs.

I was interested in the approach that the navy had worked out with Stanford and thought it was magnificent. The navy students were not all required to enroll in the same classes, but rather took courses of individual interest to them. Many of us did not have the undergraduate prerequisites for the graduate courses we took, which meant we had to work very hard to remain on a par with our fellow civilian students.

Although we were allowed to enroll in different graduate classes, we were required to attend special seminars created exclusively for us, each seminar lasting four hours and taught by a professor from a different department. Typically the professor told us about his specialty, and we told him about our backgrounds. The mix was often explosive. Some of the professors were anti-military and they had no idea about the education, assignments, character, and policies for U.S. military officers. This was particularly true of the sociology professors, who also often revealed strong anti-female attitudes about professional women that were not acceptable to our group.

All fifteen of us took heavy academic loads. Every quarter we agreed not to worry about grades because the navy was putting no pressure on us in that area. Such was our pride and competitive spirit, however, that none of us wanted to be the one with the lowest grade. We always got A's. I received my master's degree in education in June 1952, having completed graduate courses in management, philosophy, political science, psychology, and education.

⚓ ⚓ ⚓

Upon graduation from Stanford, I was assigned to be assistant director of naval personnel in the Twelfth Naval District, which had headquarters in San Francisco. The director, Commander J. W. Hager, was responsible for the geographical area of Nevada, Utah, and Northern California, which included 55,000 active and reserve personnel. We had a staff of 350 people—both military and civilian.

Commander Hager was a "mustang," as the navy refers to a former enlisted person who is selected for a commission. He had a fine mind and I found him to be an outstanding officer, although I sensed an adjustment problem at the beginning of my assignment. He never mentioned it, but I thought the tension probably arose because I was the first woman officer he ever worked with, because he knew I had advanced education, and because he had no choice but to accept me as his assistant. In May 1953, I was selected as one of two women officers to become a commander and as such was the second highest ranking woman line officer in the U.S. Navy. The other officer who was selected to the rank of commander was Katherine Dougherty.

I kept a very low profile. Whenever Commander Hager needed a report or a study done or a letter or dispatch sent to the Bureau of Personnel, I offered to do it for him. He always agreed. It became my practice to send these reports and correspondence to him ready for his signature. Later, after we had become good friends, he told me that I was the finest staff officer he had ever met. In his final fitness report about me before he retired, he wrote, "I strongly recommend that she be ordered as my replacement and I further recommend that she be considered for the number one assignment as chief of naval personnel for women."

In recommending me to be his successor, Commander Hager expressed full confidence in my abilities, but the senior officer of the Twelfth Naval District, Rear Admiral William Rodgers, felt differently. He protested that a woman officer was not capable of handling this assignment and that he would not accept me under any conditions. Of course, as assistant director I had been doing the job all along, and particularly during the absence of the director. But Admiral Rodgers was not convinced. I was familiar with this kind of prejudice. In fairness to Admiral Rodgers, no woman officer had ever held a similar assignment and this was to be one of the first "great steps forward" for a woman officer.

The admiral's message was relayed to Captain William Caspari in the Bureau of Personnel in Washington, who had the responsibility for selecting me and writing my orders to this assignment. Captain Caspari took my record to the chief of naval personnel, Vice Admiral Thomas Sprague, and asked him to review it. Captain Caspari told Admiral Sprague that I was the most qualified personnel officer in the navy. After reading my record, Admiral Sprague agreed and approved Captain Caspari sending a message under his name to Admiral Rodgers saying that if he wouldn't accept me, the Bureau of Personnel would not send a replacement. Under the circumstances, I was accepted[10]—but I don't recall that I received a warm and cordial welcome by Admiral Rodgers. I was strictly "on trial," and our relationship was limited.

Shortly after I took over as director, Admiral Rodgers was detached from the command and was replaced by Rear Admiral John Redman. What a contrast to the previous commandant! He was most cordial to me and on many occasions personally complimented me on my professional abilities.

Being director of naval personnel was a busy and high-pressure job. I was somewhat nervous in my assignment because I had never been in command of that many male officers and enlisted men. Because I wrote the fitness reports for all regular navy officers as well as reserve officers on temporary training duty, I had a lot of responsibility for male and female personnel—both military and civilian—and I also had a heavy work load.

During the time I spent in this assignment, I only had one officer who was slacking off. Although he was in a position of considerable responsibility and had a large staff, he started arriving at work late. Disciplining a lieutenant male military officer was a new experience for me, and I wasn't sure just how to handle it. I decided on a direct approach. I called him in and said, "I am very disappointed that you have been late for work every morning for the past several weeks. Up to now, you have had such a wonderful record. All your personnel are here on time. By being consistently late, you're exhibiting a very bad example of leadership. In the past I have given you excellent reports. If you don't improve, your next fitness report from me will reflect lack of responsibility and leadership."

"I'm terribly sorry," he said. "I'll never be late again." He was true to his word; in fact, after that discussion he always arrived early. Later, he was promoted to lieutenant commander, and I heard from him for twenty years.

My work in the Twelfth District was not without its lighter side. A directive came out from the chief of naval personnel stating that all naval officers of the rank of commander and above were required to have swords. The directive did not specify that women officers of that rank were exempted but I felt it logical that we were, so I did not wear one. My staff kept asking me, "Where is your sword?"

One day, the joke took an unusual turn. Frequently on Fridays, after work, my staff officers and I would have cocktails at the nearby officers' club. When they asked me to join them on this particular Friday, I saw nothing unusual about it. However, instead of having our drinks in the main bar, we met in a separate club room. When I inquired about the reason, they told me there was a large private party in the regular room so the manager suggested we use this smaller room. Soon, Admiral Redman and other senior officers stopped by. The admiral said he was attending a party a little later, but seeing all of us, he wondered if he could join us for a drink. We welcomed him. By this time, the room was filled with staff officers, wives, and civilian friends. I thought they were en route to the big party in the main bar.

Suddenly, a ship's bell rang out. Just as I was wondering what it was all about, two women junior officers came in the door wearing their uniforms and white gloves and carrying what looked like a sword. The admiral turned to me and said, "Commander

Quick, we felt your uniform without a sword was not 'regulation,' so we are presenting to you a sword which reflects your femininity." He then presented me the "sword" in a red leather scabbard covered with multi-colored sequins, saying, "Now draw the sword." I pulled on the handle with vigor, and out came a small knife!

I considered this surprise an expression of their affection for me, and I was both amused by and appreciative of the incident. I fully understand that from our current vantage point, the giving of such a "feminine" sword could be seen as a "put-down." But given the times and the feeling of camaraderie and good will among my colleagues, I was amused and felt no sense of insult.

Commander Winifred Quick Collins receiving a sword from Rear Admiral John Redman. Official U.S. Navy photograph.

⚓ ⚓ ⚓

I remained in my post as director until 1956, when I was being considered for an assignment to the staff of the senior naval command in Europe—with headquarters in London—which included the Sixth Fleet, located in the Mediterranean. I was ordered to Washington to be interviewed. Normally, a male officer would be sent to that command without any fuss or fitness record, but because I was a woman I had to be interviewed by about eight senior officers. In 1956, male chauvinism was alive and well.

I thought this interrogation was ridiculous and I said to the lieutenant commander woman officer who accompanied me on my interviews, "If I could just wear a fig leaf, I wouldn't have to go through all these interviews." Although I had an outstanding record, senior male officers who interviewed me obviously had a hard time accepting the fact that I—or any woman officer—could be as competent as a male officer. I passed the endless interviews and inspections and was issued orders to the London Navy Command. Upon my detachment from the Twelfth Naval District, Admiral Redman wrote a most favorable fitness report.

Before I left the states, I wanted to see my father, who was then living in Los Angeles. I went to his home and found that he had been taken to the hospital earlier that day with pneumonia. When I got to the hospital I found him in a coma. I held his hand and said, "This is Boots. I want to talk to you. If you can hear me, squeeze my hand." As I talked, he squeezed my hand, and I knew he could understand me as I tried to comfort him.

It was a deeply emotional time for me as I knew he was dying. I did not want him to die alone, but I could not delay my departure. I called my brother Larry, who was stationed in Hawaii, to see if he could come. Because of an important flying examination in the next few days, he could not leave. It was a great disappointment to me that my father died alone, at the age of 93, while I was at sea, en route to London.

I had been ordered to travel on the U.S.S. *America*, a passenger ship of U.S. Lines. I was slated to share a cabin with two air force women officers, but when I got on board, the steward took me to a large, beautiful stateroom on the top deck. I felt there had been a mistake and called the ship's purser. He told me that there was no mistake. The president of U.S. Lines, Giles Stedman, whom I had met in San Francisco at navy social affairs, had noticed my name on the manifest and changed my room. He left flowers in the stateroom with a kind message: "I think you will enjoy these quarters much more—smooth sailing." It was my first ship voyage and my first trip to Europe. In spite of my sadness over losing my father, I had a wonderful time and met some delightful passengers.

The day after I arrived in London, I reported to the command and my new boss, a captain. He said, "I'd like you to go to Paris tomorrow to attend a joint army, navy, and air force committee meeting. But I don't want you to make any commitments for this command."

"Captain, I don't think you need worry about my making a commitment, as I don't even know the name of the committee," I said. "Could you tell me something about it so that I can be a little better informed?" He wandered off without making any comment.

With much trepidation, knowing I was to represent my command, I went to Paris the next day. I noticed two generals at the head table. I knew that I had to give an explanation immediately, so I said, "Gentlemen, I arrived from the States yesterday and was told to attend this meeting. I must say that under this short notice, I am totally embarrassed that I know nothing about this committee and my responsibility." Possibly because I was a woman, the officers were most gracious. They asked me to sit between them and said that they would brief me as we went along. The committee was a very important one and represented agreements between U.S. Forces and each of our North Atlantic Treaty Organization (NATO) countries where our U.S. troops were stationed.

Three months later, the committee met at our navy headquarters in London, and I was chairman. By then I had done my homework and was able to run the meeting with 100 officer attendees.

My assignment in London had many responsibilities. I was senior assistant to the chief of staff for administration, senior member responsible for the funds of all the officers' and enlisted men's clubs throughout Europe, navy member of the Joint Provost Marshal Board (which reviewed infractions by military personnel in violation of NATO agreements with a country in which an infraction had occurred), and member of the European Command Joint Armed Forces Coordinating Committee. I was also responsible for planning details for all VIP visitors to this command.

I was fortunate in having several assignments that took me out of London almost every month. At the completion of one of my committee meetings in Naples, one of the attendees, an army colonel, asked me if I had ever been on the Amalfi Drive, the road that led across the mountains overlooking the Mediterranean, which was reputed to be gorgeous. I said I hadn't. He explained that there was a trip that we could take starting Saturday morning with a driver-guide and that we could be back Sunday in time to catch a plane back to our separate commands in Paris and London.

It sounded wonderful. I said that I'd like to join him but he had to understand that I was paying for all my own expenses, which involved staying overnight in Sorrento. It was a fantastic trip, and he was a delightful companion. We arrived at a lovely old hotel in Sorrento, and after a late dinner we went to our separate rooms. About 11 P.M. my phone rang; it was my traveling companion. He said, "I'm freezing in this marble hotel."

"I'm sorry to hear that, as I'm very cozy," I said. "But I have an idea. When you hear a light tap on your door, open it cautiously."

He was very much intrigued. When he opened his door, he saw the fattest little toothless woman in Italy. She held out two hot water bottles. "For you, signore," she said, smiling her best smile.

The colonel and I had breakfast at the appointed hour the next morning. "I have never known a woman who had such a warped sense of humor," he said. We continued to be friends and I heard from him for many years after I left London.

On one of my trips for a committee meeting in Paris, I was called away to answer a phone call from London. When I answered, I heard the aide of my command's admiral tell me that the admiral would like to speak to me. I felt sure that I was going to get a reprimand for something I had done, as the admiral was not given to light conversation. "I have a confidential message from the secretary of the navy," the admiral said. "You have been selected as the top navy woman, the next chief of naval personnel for women. Congratulations." The admiral then hung up the phone.

It is a navy tradition that when an officer is detached from a command that a party be given for him or her. It never happened in this case, although I was going to the top job for a woman in the U.S. Navy. But the staff captains gave me a lovely luncheon and told me that they were going to auction off my orders as they were all envious that I could leave this command. I cautioned them that it was great to auction off my orders, but not a one of them could pass the physical for my assignment.

Prior to my departure from London, Dame Robertson, former commandant of the British Wrens,[11] gave me a beautiful party which many members of Parliament attended. Two royal princesses who were Wren officers were present at the party, along with some members of Parliament. My association with the Wrens had been delightful, as I had visited their training school for enlisted Wrens and had enjoyed many social occasions with their officers.

When I sailed home on the U.S.S. *United States*, I was one of three military women to share a very small cabin. I had been on board only a short time when a steward gave me a written message that the captain of the ship wished to see me on a confidential matter. He greeted me in his quarters. "I have a message that you have been selected as the top woman in the navy," he said. "I want to offer you a beautiful suite on the top deck. I married a WAVE. Under no circumstances could I permit you to share a small cabin. If I did, I'd probably be divorced."

I moved to a beautiful suite without the knowledge of my former roommates. I enjoyed meeting the other passengers, and my entire voyage was delightful. It was easy for me to adjust to the calm and elegance of the voyage across the Atlantic, but I knew that the serenity of the trip would be in sharp contrast to the turbulence of the journey that I would be taking as number one woman in the navy.

---

[1] When they went home in August 1946 after demonstrating superb administrative talents in the demobilization effort, I was able to get a letter of commendation for their outstanding performance.

[2] Bureau of Naval Personnel, Navy Department, Washington, D.C.

[3] Career male officers and enlisted personnel at each level of the regular navy are required to have a certain type of sea duty, but they cannot be kept at sea for their entire career because the navy needs the right balance between navy male officers at sea and those assigned to shore billet for its rotation system to work. Some navy men feared that women having shore jobs would interfere with the ability of navy men to come back to shore duty and be with their families, but no problem existed because there were sufficient shore billets.

[4] U.S. Cong., Senate, *Women's Armed Services Integration Act of 1947*, Hearings before the Committee on Armed Services, 80th Cong., 1st Sess., 1947, p. 94.

[5] Ibid., p. 95.

[6] Ibid., p. 95.

[7] This was a statutory restriction.

[8] U.S. Congress, House of Representatives, *To Establish the Women's Army Corps in the Regular Army, To Authorize the Enlistment and Appointment of Women in the Regular Navy and Marine Corps and the Naval and Marine Corps Reserve, and for Other Purposes,* Hearings before Subcommittee No. 3, Organization and Mobilization, of the Committee on Armed Services, 80th Cong., 2nd Sess., 1948, p. 5604.

[9] The "W" signified "Women."

[10] As the first woman officer to hold the job as director, I was interviewed in December of 1953 by the *Christian Science Monitor.*

[11] The Wrens are a women's auxiliary to the British Navy. The men and women of the British royal family usually hold a commission in the British navy.

five

NUMBER ONE
NAVY WOMAN

My new position promised to be the most challenging professional assignment of my life. I looked forward to my work with both excitement and apprehension. As one who had risen from the ranks, I was elated and honored to have reached the top—that is, the top for a *woman*. But as someone who had been in London—away from women's personnel matters—for a few years, I was not aware of some of the extraordinary problems I was about to face. It took me only a few days to fully appreciate how difficult it would be to solve them.

My predecessor was Captain Louise Wilde, a friend from my days at Smith College. When I became captain, she had to revert to the rank of commander because of the legal restriction of permitting only one woman officer at a time to hold the temporary rank of captain while serving in that position. No male naval officer demoted from a top job lost his rank in this manner. It was a terrible and unfair adjustment for her. She had been ill for the previous two years and, consequently, left me with many serious problems.

My other close friend from Smith days was Winifred Love. Already assigned in the Bureau of Personnel as the woman officer detailer,[1] she was great comfort for me to have in that position. My staff consisted of my first deputy and two yeomen. We covered a broad territory in trying to do everything, including making plans and policies for navy women. My first deputy, Commander Eleanor Sowers, had also been deputy to Captain Wilde. Sowers was with me until 1961, after which she was replaced by Commander Viola Sanders, who had been on the Antarctica staff in Washington, D.C. My third deputy was Commander Rita Lenahan. All of my deputies performed their duties magnificently. I sent them out on speaking and inspection tours both because I thought they needed the experience and because I needed their input. After working with me, first Viola Sanders and then Rita Lenahan became assistant chief of naval personnel for women.

The clear lines of the official management structure at the Bureau of Personnel provided no clue to understanding the administrative complexity of my job. The chief of naval personnel was at the top of the bureau, and below him was a deputy, a legal counsel, and a special assistant for leadership. In addition, there were eleven assistant chiefs, each of whom headed a division: plans, personnel control, education and training, naval reserve, records, performance, morale, finance, chief of chaplains, navy women (which was my job), and property management. We were each referred to as "directors" or "chiefs" of our specialty.

Unofficially, I was called "director for navy women" or "chief for navy women." Frequently, the press asked me who was the "chief" if I was the "assistant chief." I had to tell them that the two titles referred to the same position. The other assistant chiefs had a similar problem of identification in describing the titles of their divisions.

An administrative feature that made my job difficult was that all of the male officers—both admirals and captains—were senior to me. As far as rank was concerned, I held a subordinate status to my "equals." The successful accomplishment of my objectives meant dealing with each of these admirals or senior captains. It was a confusing and time-consuming management structure.

Captain Winifred Quick, newly appointed chief of naval personnel for women. Official U.S. Navy photograph.

Every proposal I made regarding the total number of women (in both regular and reserve status), their recruitment, their education and training, their performance, their promotion, or their morale, all needed to be coordinated with at least one of the assistant chiefs.

I discovered early that my first chief of the Bureau of Personnel, Vice Admiral James Halloway, Jr., would never tell me what to do—not, it appeared, because he thought I had no need for guidance, but because no one was particularly certain what I *should* do. My boss never said, for instance, "I want you to look into recruitment," or "I want you to look into this or that." I had to determine what was needed and then try to win support from him and other senior officers for any changes I wanted.

So many problems for navy women cried out for immediate resolution that every year I compiled a long list of goals I wanted to accomplish. My major problem was determining which items on the list were the highest priority. In my job as assistant chief of naval personnel for women, I set standards for the performance of duties and dealt with discipline, housing, uniforming, promotion, retirement, education, and publicity. I had responsibilities for encouraging the assignment officer to find appropriate assignments for women through the rotation of navy women personnel so that they could gain more knowledge as they rose in rank or rating. I also requested evaluations of professional skills and qualities of navy women so assignment officers could find positions that would match their abilities.

In my five years as "number one," I worked with many high-level male officials, many of whom were indifferent to having women in the navy and so at first resisted my suggestions to make them a more integral part of it. But most senior officers were supportive, and it did not take me too long to identify which ones. Persuasion was an important part of my job.

Soon after taking over my new assignment, I made a courtesy call to Admiral Arleigh Burke, chief of naval operations (CNO), who was known as "Thirty-one-knot Burke."[2] I had never met him until that moment. He got up from his chair, came around to the front of his desk, and stared intently at me. "You have the prettiest blue eyes I have ever seen," he said.

Caught by surprise, since I was trying to act according to the highest standards of military protocol, I said, "Dear God, now what do I do, Admiral?"

He burst out in laughter, and then he got serious. "I am very proud of you," he said. "I know your record. I am happy that I am chief of naval operations during the time you're going to be in charge of all the navy women. If you have any problems, you can come directly to me anytime."

We became instant friends. He gave me a lovely welcoming cocktail party with the senior echelon of the navy—both civilians and officers. It was there that I first met Mrs. Burke, who became most helpful to me in my new post. She volunteered to accompany me (and did) when I went on inspection trips for navy women.

I called on Secretary of the Navy Thomas Gates, who was also wonderfully gracious to me. "Captain," he said, "I want you to know that there is no chain of command from your desk to mine. If you have a problem you can't handle or you find a lack of cooperation from some of the senior male officers, please come and discuss it with me. Are you having any trouble with any of your programs?"

"Mr. Secretary, I'm having trouble with just about every single program," I replied.

"Well, I'll tell you what I'll do," he said. "I'll invite some of the key admirals to a luncheon, and we'll have a cocktail. And when we sit down to lunch, I'm going to turn to you and say, 'Now, are you having any problems?'" And he did just that, allowing me to describe my problems at the appropriate moment. The secretary would say to an admiral, "Well, Jack, can't you do something about that?" Or, "Tom, why can't you settle this?" Secretary Gates was a great source of much-needed support and backing.

Shortly after I made the courtesy calls, I was scheduled to hold a press conference, something I had not done before. I had been told by many navy people that the press did not like the military and that the women reporters, in particular, would be very difficult to deal with during an interview. Also I was cautioned to speak very carefully because the press delighted in misquoting military personnel. I was unsure of my ability to handle this situation, but finally decided that a direct approach might be best. In front of reporters from newspapers and radio and television stations, I opened the meeting by saying, "This is the first press conference I've ever held, and I am very nervous about meeting all you professionals because you are so knowledgeable."

I then described my predicament: "The navy often has a unique way of selecting officers for assignments. In my case, I have until quite recently been in the navy's senior military command dealing with interservice NATO problems and therefore have no up-to-date information about the navy women's program. I hope you will bear with me until I become more knowledgeable. Given a few weeks, I will become better informed about the status of navy women and will be happy to see you again and answer all of your questions." I was being honest; I was really uninformed. Although I was nervous that I might say something that I would regret, my press conference worked out beautifully. The women reporters were very pleasant to me that day and when they returned later. I had great rapport with the press women; and some of them became my close and personal friends.

It was clear to me at the very beginning in my new post that the situation for navy women was even worse than I had suspected, in part because of the extended illness of my predecessor. I had a big job ahead.

I needed to work on the problems of poor quality in recruiting for both officers and enlisted women, impediments to career development, inadequate housing and recreation, low morale, poor self-image, and negative public attitudes.[3]

After studying the problems, I realized that the low morale and negative attitudes were caused by many factors. Among the most important were poor living conditions in the barracks; lack of recreational facilities; inadequate petty officer leadership; faulty selectivity at the recruiting level; a high ratio of enlisted men to the smaller number of women (about a hundred to one); higher educational achievements of enlisted women compared to enlisted men; uncertainty of enlisted women regarding their role in the navy; and the sexist attitudes of males in the navy as well as in civilian life. I also realized that the problems were interrelated, and that solving one would likely lead to solutions to others.

I gave much attention to the dreadful housing situation which, at least on the enlisted personnel level, was even worse for men than for women. Men had large dormitory-style rooms, "gang" showers (large shower rooms), and toilets without doors in addition to all the problems the enlisted women had. The enlisted barracks for both women and men were uninsulated wooden structures mostly built in the 1941–1942 period, when they were thought of as "temporary," but they were still being used in 1957. They were cold in the winter, but resembled "furnaces" in the hot climates during the summer, because air conditioning was not available. Since these structures were possible fire traps, fire drills were frequent. Although the drills were held at reasonable hours, they were nevertheless disruptive. The only saving grace these barracks had was that they had been built at a time when the number of enlisted personnel was large, so that in the postwar years there was more space for the occupants than there had been when the barracks were new.

The women's barracks consisted of cubicles with single double-bunk beds. They had a number of separate showers in one large shower room and toilets with separate stalls and doors. There were no kitchens or closets. Clothing and personal items were kept in footlockers—one for each person. There was one— usually inadequate—recreation room. The size of the barracks varied. Usually there were fifty enlisted women per barracks.

I tackled head-on the problem of improving the barracks. I went to the civil engineers—the construction people—to discuss plans for building new ones as well as remodeling the old ones. Plans for both the new and the remodeled barracks had separate rooms rather than cubicles. I recommended that provisions be made for air conditioners, kitchens, refrigerators, stoves, washers, dryers, hair dryers, televisions, and radios. Plans also included expanded recreational areas. I was able to get our recreational department to furnish radios, televisions, phonographs with dance records, newspapers, books, and magazines—all paid for out of non-tax dollars. During my time as assistant director, every one of the existing barracks for enlisted navy women in all shore activities in the United States and Hawaii was either remodeled or was a new construction. Living conditions for navy women were much improved and the enlisted women appreciated the change. In the Washington area, all enlisted personnel—army, navy, and air force—eventually lived at Fort Myer in new modern brick dormitories with excellent inside facilities and a wide variety of recreational activities available.

Oddly—or maybe not so oddly—the improved housing arrangements for navy women led to improved housing arrangements for navy men, since it was not long afterwards that newly constructed or renovated barracks with private rooms were also built for navy enlisted men, as well as new bachelor officers' quarters for men and women.

Housing conditions had been bad not only because of the decrepit age of the barracks but also because of the particular mix of people. I found that senior petty officers and new recruits were housed in the same barracks—a situation that brought together two different age groups with vastly different personal interests and lifestyles.

Luckily, the living quarters of women officers varied. In metropolitan areas, women officers did not live in bachelor officers' quarters but had private apartments. In some instances—particularly overseas (e.g., London, Naples, Paris, and cities in West Germany)—enlisted women also rented their own private apartments. I appealed to my boss, the chief of the Bureau of Personnel, to authorize the senior petty officers stationed in Washington, D.C., to be given rent and food allowances so that they could live outside the barracks. I thought that granting such allowances would give the senior women a far more pleasant life. The vice admiral gave me a very strong "no" to my request and did not offer to discuss the subject, so I solicited the help of Secretary Gates. I explained the barracks situation to him, and he was very concerned. "I'm surprised the admiral isn't interested in the morale and living conditions of the enlisted personnel," he said.

I answered that in my view, the vice admiral was not concerned with the living conditions of navy women, but instead was interested in appearing before Congress and becoming a great statesman. In his way of looking at things, navy women were a minor matter, while in mine, they were of utmost importance. I could not, however, solve the housing problem without his help. I recognized that my remarks could be seen as very "unmilitary," since it is inappropriate for someone to criticize a senior in front of his or her superior. But the living conditions of enlisted personnel constituted a terrible problem, and one I felt it was my responsibility to solve.

Secretary Gates decided that he would like to see an enlisted barracks. "I'll have my aide call the chief's aide and say that I would like to inspect a nearby barracks. And as an afterthought, I'll say I'd like to see an enlisted women's barracks."

An inspection date was set soon after our meeting. The inspection party consisted of Secretary Gates, me, the vice admiral of the Bureau of Personnel and his deputy (a rear admiral), and two aides. As planned, we toured the women's barracks, and the secretary said, "Admiral, the captain says that if she wouldn't get caught, she'd like to burn down this barracks, and I'd like to join her. However, this would be very bad publicity for the navy if we were caught. I wonder if we could relieve the crowded condition by letting the senior petty officers live outside. Is there any way that might be done?"

"Oh, yes, Mr. Secretary," the admiral said, practically bowing and scraping. "I can handle that easily. If Captain Quick will give me a list of those senior petty officers who are living in the barracks, I will authorize them to live in the community."

When I said goodbye to Secretary Gates and thanked him, he gave me a big wink. He later became secretary of defense, and we always maintained a cordial relationship. He was a wonderful human being and a great statesman. I often told him that I hoped he would become our president.

When I traveled to shore installations around the country, I told commanding officers that in Washington, D.C., chiefs and first class were authorized subsistence allowances so they could live in the community. Commanding officers in other parts of the country soon followed the Washington example, but often only after some gentle arm twisting on my part. One case in particular is worth noting because of the extraordinarily wretched housing conditions. At Patuxent Naval Base in Maryland, I found that enlisted navy women—mostly Hospital Corps—were living in some of the worst barracks I had seen. The commanding officer had even assigned a male patrol to circle the women's barracks every fifteen minutes, making the place seem like a prison. I talked informally with the enlisted women, who complained about their dismal housing arrangements. Also, as Hospital Corps personnel, they were working seventy-two hours a week in rotating shifts and then having their sleep disturbed by barracks noise. And when they were off work, they had no recreation. I made a list of their grievances, and I went to the commanding officer.

"These are human beings," I said to him. "You can't treat them like prisoners. I will remove every single Hospital Corps enlisted woman from your command if you do not improve their living and recreational facilities."

"Oh, no, no," he said. "We need these women."

"Then you have to bring up your standards for women's barracks. You have to provide recreational facilities and remove the patrols."

I learned from talking with him that there was nothing negative about his attitudes towards navy women. Because this was his first encounter with them, he was simply unaware of the morale problem his rules were creating. He had never even visited their barracks and was under the impression that having a guard around their housing was a form of protection, not detention. Once informed of the realities, he was willing to make the appropriate changes. And when he did what he promised, morale soared.

Gradually, in each command, all the chiefs and the first class ranks were permitted to have their own civilian apartments, if available, thus contributing to an overall better morale among senior women in the navy. At the same time, I recognized that a few of the very best of the chiefs needed to live in the barracks for a short tour and serve as leaders and act as supervisors of the young women when they arrived in the barracks. Group living required rules, and some of the young women had problems in dealing with them. The petty officers living among them could quickly solve potential problems before they became serious. In exchange for volunteering to live in the barracks, they would enhance their record and receive promotion points.

⚓ ⚓ ⚓

Lack of career advancement was another big problem for navy women—both officer and enlisted—in 1957. Processes for promotion, selection, and education all impeded women's progress in developing their careers. We never heard the term *glass ceiling* back in the 1950s and 1960s, but we understood everything there was to know about it.[4] We faced legal and policy barriers in promotion, job assignment, educational opportunities, and retirement.

As Chapter 4 describes, the Women's Armed Forces Integration Act allowed only one woman line officer captain at a time, and this was regarded as a temporary assignment. The highest permanent grade for women authorized by the law was commander. The number of regular navy women commanders and lieutenant commanders was not to exceed ten percent and twenty percent respectively of the total number of regular navy women line officers on the active list. (In contrast, the law governing male officer promotion was based on a percentage of the *combined* number of active duty and reserves—a much larger base.)

The law also prescribed terms of service for promotion purposes as follows: ensign, three years; lieutenant (jg), three years; lieutenant, four years; and lieutenant commander, four years. Lieutenant (jgs) who completed seven years of active commissioned service and lieutenants who completed thirteen years and were not then on a promotion list to the next higher grade were required to separate from the navy. This separation was designed to parallel the "forced attrition" feature for male officers, where the rationale was that the men so separated were still young enough to find other career opportunities in civilian fields. The problem for navy women officers was that we had not reached the 500 maximum that was permitted by law. On January 1, 1953, for example, there were only 281 regular navy women officers on the active list. In 1957, the number had risen to only 300.[5] Competent women officers could not be promoted unless there were vacancies.

Louise Wilde, my predecessor as assistant chief, had sought to provide some solution to the obstacle of promotion for navy women officers by trying to increase the number of regular navy women line officers on the active list, speeding up the process whereby eligible naval reservists on active duty could be appointed as commissioned officers of the regular navy. (The movement from reserve to active status is known as "augmentation.") She also sought to get Congress to amend Public Law 625 to permit flexibility in the rank percentages it designated. In January 1955, the chief of naval personnel forwarded to the judge advocate general (JAG) legislative proposals designed to achieve her purpose. On June 15, 1956, the persistent efforts of Captain Wilde were successful. Congress passed Public Law 585, which amended Public Law 625.

The amendments provided that when the authorized number of line commanders is less than the maximum permitted by law, which is ten percent of the number of women officers on the active list of the line, the difference may be applied to increase the authorized number of line lieutenant commanders, which was fixed at twenty percent. This provision was similar to a legislative provision for male officers and permitted flexibility in the distribution of women officers in these two grades.

The amendments also permitted for a period of four years following enactment of this legislation the selective retention (until completion of fifteen years of active commission service) of those lieutenants who would otherwise be separated from the service after thirteen years of active commissioned service. Each officer concerned was given an opportunity to indicate whether or not she desired retention. This change gave lieutenants selected for retention additional opportunities to be considered for promotion.

In 1957, my objective as captain was to set in motion procedures to bring about a change in the basic law affecting the number and ranks of navy women. I recognized, however, that this would be a long and tedious process.[6]

At the same time, I tried to increase the number of regular navy women officers on active duty and was somewhat successful in this endeavor. As head of women in the regular navy, active reserves, and inactive reserves, I proposed that these women be trained and assigned to jobs similar to ones assigned the regular women on active duty. Because the navy had a policy for the inactive male reservist, I felt we needed to establish a similar policy for female reservists, particularly so they could build up retirement eligibility. When I took over in 1957, there were a limited number of women in the inactive naval reserve. It was necessary to develop a program giving women reservists training in jobs they would fill in a national emergency. When I left in 1962, we had an active training program filling this need.

Speeding up the augmentation process of moving a woman officer from reserve to regular navy status was one way I increased the number of women officers. This change involved allowing the college graduates (ensigns) to join the regular navy much sooner than the previous policy allowed. It permitted reservists to apply immediately for augmentation instead of waiting a year, thus accelerating the number of active duty regular officers and increasing promotion opportunities in lieutenant commander and commander grades. Prospective women officers were commissioned upon graduation from the Women's Officer Indoctrination School at Newport.[7]

I was able to gradually raise the number of regular navy women officers on active duty but I was not willing to sacrifice quality for quantity in the recruiting effort. I knew that if we improved quality, then quantity would soon follow. I put in very strict selection standards for officer personnel at the recruiting level, determined to accept only the best candidates even though it resulted in smaller numbers. The emphasis on quality rather than quantity was not without its dangers, however. It was obvious to me that we could not continue to have an officer school for the small number of women officers we were recruiting. I knew I had to come up with a solution before the school was closed down.

In 1958, we commissioned only nine women officers to go to the Women's Officer Indoctrination School at Newport. Procurement was the problem, since there were too few qualified applicants. I didn't need anybody to tell me that we couldn't afford to have a staff of nine there for nine officer candidates, so I called the head of the navy Nurse Corps, Captain Ruth A. Houghton, and asked if she would like to send her prospective Nurse Corps ensigns to the Women's Officer Indoctrination School. Prior to this time, nurses had been commissioned as ensigns and sent directly to hospital duty without any military indoctrination. Captain Houghton was delighted with the idea. She understood that the nurses' morale and personal sense of belonging to the navy would greatly improve if the nurses could share this officer indoctrination with the women line and other staff officers. It turned out to be a fine idea. The navy nurses learned about the navy, and their morale increased because they felt they were part of the regular navy. Moreover, many friendships were established between the two groups. It was a life-saver for me because it gave me enough students to keep the officer school open.

By this time, the curriculum for navy women officer candidates was far more developed than the curriculum I had encountered in those early days at Smith College. Now, the navy women received much the same basic training as college men who became ensigns, learning about navy history, ships, aircraft, leadership, protocol, and etiquette. Women learned enough to develop a common background with these college men who became ensigns, although they did not receive the operational knowledge about seagoing skills.

⚓ ⚓ ⚓

I discovered that recruiting and retaining talented navy women was to a large measure influenced by morale and self-esteem. If enlisted women felt good about being a part of the navy, they would apply for reenlistment. In order to obtain more information about what navy women officers and some enlisted women thought of themselves and what they liked or disliked about navy life, I sent out a questionnaire with the following questions:

1. What kind of women join the navy?
2. If women are trained in the navy and eventually get out, isn't this a waste of money and education?
3. When women do leave the navy, do they find their experiences in the navy provide them with a better job in civilian life?
4. Why should I think about a military career if I hope to marry some day?

5. How different are the jobs you have had in the navy from what you could do as a civilian?

6. What is meant by "naval leadership"?

7. Are women in the service respected by other military personnel?

8. What supervision and guidance do young women in the service receive?

9. What business and social contacts do women in the navy have in the local communities?

10. What types of jobs and assignments do service women have?

11. What are their educational opportunities? Chances for advancement?

12. What would prompt a college graduate to apply for a commission?

13. How do mothers feel about their daughters joining the navy?

I received a tremendous number of responses, then targeted the most evident problems. For instance, I learned that in recruitment, we weren't getting the quality of talent that we needed. I went to the director of recruitment and said, "I just don't understand why we're not getting the numbers and quality of women officers and enlisted women I want in the navy."

He replied in surprise: "You aren't?"

Exploring the problem together, we learned that navy recruiting success was evaluated by a point system in which every recruiting station would get so many points for the number of *male* officers and enlisted personnel it signed up, but no points for the number of *female* officers and enlisted personnel. The system was changed to give equal credit for the recruitment of women.

I also learned through the questionnaires that to an eighteen-year-old, a four-year enlistment seems like a lifetime. "By then, I'll be too old to get married," some young women wrote. It was because of attitudes like this that strictly equal treatment did not always work for the women. I decided that if we wanted to recruit more talented women, we needed to shorten the enlistment requirement. Because enlisted navy men had a four-year service requirement, it was tough persuading the navy to approve a three-year enlistment requirement for women, but I succeeded. This change increased our recruiting tremendously. The shortened term did not apply to navy women officers since they were commissioned as reservists. Under my new policy the navy reserve women could apply one year earlier for a regular navy commission upon graduation from the Women's Officer Indoctrination School. Women officers could resign at any time unless they had further graduate education provided by the navy, in which case they were obligated for the same amount of time as they spent on graduate work.

I also learned from the questionnaires, as well as from my own observation and experience, that navy women faced great difficulties in developing their careers because of the lack of a career ladder. In order for navy women to advance in their careers, they had to be given good assignments, which they often could not get because of a variety of obstacles that were placed in their way. I learned about one in particular soon after I took over as chief. For some reason I could not fathom, women officers of the rank of commander or lieutenant commander were being consistently rejected by commanding officers. They would at first be accepted by the commanding officers but later in the process they would be rejected. If these women could not get assigned, there would be no place for them in the navy.

I could not understand why such qualified women were being rejected—until I investigated. I learned that in all assignments in the higher ranks, a security clearance of "secret" or higher was required. Women in those grades were not being accepted by the commands to which they were ordered because the Office of Intelligence did not provide to those commands appropriate security clearance for any women naval officers. Deeply concerned, I set up an appointment to speak to the assistant chief of naval personnel for performance, who worked with the Office of Naval Intelligence and had classified information on investigations and discipline problems affecting all naval personnel. When I told him my problem, he said he thought he knew what was happening.

The Office of Naval Intelligence was responsible for the security clearance level for all officers. By navy directive, naval intelligence security officers were supposed to make decisions regarding the reliability and level of security clearance of the navy personnel. However, instead of complying with the directive, the intelligence officers were sending excerpts of their reports to the commanding officers rather than issuing a security clearance. These reports contained such notations as the fact that two women officers were living together, or that they had been hugging their women friends at airports—the implication being that these women were lesbians, an allegation which, if true, would by navy regulations of the times have led to an automatic court martial and a dishonorable discharge. After furnishing this kind of information, the investigators were leaving the decision on security clearance up to the commanding officer—rather than making the decision themselves.

After conferring with the captain in charge of performance, I asked him if he would set up a conference with the representatives of the Office of Naval Intelligence. On the day of our meeting, I was astounded to find that nine civilian men from that office had arrived for my conference. That number made me confident that my meeting was being carefully considered by the intelligence officers. I had known the women officers who were being rejected for many years, and they were not lesbians. Before a man or woman was even accepted to the navy—as officer or enlisted—the intelligence officers checked his or her background. They went to the high school principal, teachers, college professors, and community people and asked about the kind of individual this person was, including questions about sex habits, alcohol consumption, social habits, and reputation. If there had been a security problem, the navy would not have accepted the person in the first place. The background investigation made it highly unlikely for a lesbian or homosexual to be accepted into the navy at this time.

"Gentlemen," I said, "I have a serious problem that concerns procedures you are using in your security reports to commanding officers. I have confirmed evidence that you are not sending them your security clearance of the senior women officers but are instead sending information that implies that these women are lesbians. This is in conflict with a navy directive. You are violating regulations by sending information and imposing on commanding officers the decision as to the security clearance they should give a prospective candidate. That is not their responsibility.

"This is my proposal to you. Within one week from today, I want every one of these officers to receive a security report from your office. If the report is derogatory, then you must submit documented facts so that court martial proceedings can be initiated at once. I have personally known all of the officers in question for years. It is my judgment that you are evaluating them by cultural standards for males, which are different from those for females. When you see two females hugging or sharing an apartment, it is totally wrong to conclude that they are lesbians.

"If I do not hear from you about these women in one week, I will go to the secretary of the navy and tell him how you have been violating his directives regarding clearance procedures for women personnel."

I concluded by thanking them for giving me their time and requesting they advise the assistant chief of performance of their decision in one week. Their options were clear: Either assign a clearance or initiate court martial proceedings.

As a result, every woman officer received a high level security clearance within the week.

I assume that the offensive procedure had been deliberately devised because some men did not want women in the navy, and such a policy made it difficult for women to get good jobs. But I did not want to waste time worrying about the reason. I just wanted the problem resolved, and it was—much to my satisfaction.

While I did not find lesbianism itself to be a problem for the navy, I did find that the mind-set of intelligence officials toward it often created a problem for navy women. For example, I learned that two male agents interrogated many new navy enlisted women and accused them of holding hands with another enlisted woman. The questions and accusations of these intelligence officers implied that such conduct was proof that the woman was a lesbian and unfit for the navy. The investigators were using strong-arm scare tactics on these young eighteen-year-olds, many of whom were so intimidated by the tough questioning that they gave up and signed a "confession," then received dishonorable discharges from the navy—marring their lives. In 1957, I got the policy modified to require that a woman officer be present at any interrogation of an enlisted navy woman by the intelligence agent. The male interviewers fought me tooth and nail about that. "A woman officer will only interfere," they said.

"She won't say a word," I countered. "She's just going to be present." Sure enough, a woman's mere presence modified their interrogation procedures completely. No scare tactics were used after the implementation of the new policy. In fact, a remarkable development occurred: The dismissals for "lesbianism" stopped dead in their tracks. If there were lesbians dismissed from the navy in the period I was assistant chief of naval personnel for women, I personally can't recall a single case. The practice of falsely and illegally accusing women of being lesbians was not only an unfair tactic, but the resulting dismissals were costly to the navy and to the accused, but innocent, individuals.

⚓ ⚓ ⚓

My dealings with intelligence officials were not the only obstacles in career development for navy women that I had to solve. Another was the matter of rotation between assignments after two to three years on a job. This matter had been a subject of concern as early as 1948 when Congress considered legislation to provide for women to be in the regular military services. The 1948 rotation directive which I developed for navy women (except for sea duty), following that of navy men, provided a new assignment in U.S. Navy shore facilities after two to three years in an assignment in the states, or after two years in an assignment overseas. Each new assignment represented increased responsibility and skill.

I devised a career ladder for women in which certain assignments were required for promotion. My thought was to establish the equivalent of "sea duty" for certain key assignments which would provide needed leadership roles for the more senior women officers and petty officers. These assignments—enlisted barracks duty for senior petty officers and recruiting duty and instructor duty at our Recruit Training School and at our Women's Officer Indoctrination School in Newport—had not previously attracted the best officers and enlisted personnel. These assignments were crucial to the success of the navy women's program and needed to be filled by highly qualified women. The new promotion plan encouraged both officer and enlisted navy women to request these assignments, once it was clear that these jobs were the equivalent of "sea duty" for men, and it greatly strengthened the leadership role of navy women.

Another way I was able to expand career opportunities for women was to utilize the talents of women officers who were already working in the Bureau of Personnel. In this way I could use these especially selected officers as a valuable information resource, and at the same time advance their promotion opportunities and coordinate plans for other talented navy women. I tried to choose women who were intelligent, knowledgeable, and personable but who were innovative in their determination to coordinate career plans for women officers and senior petty officers.

For example, there were two women officers in the Bureau of Personnel who made the assignments for all navy women—both officer and enlisted. Each officer had to coordinate every assignment with the various male specialty desks in that division. There were rank desks to deal with personnel matters in particular ranks, and command desks responsible for personnel matters in different commands. Commander Winifred Love, who served as my assignment officer, knew all the key male officers involved in assigning officers and personally went to each one to describe the individual records of women officers who could be assigned to various posts, because in many cases, the decision-makers in personnel might not realize the availability of qualified women officers. Acting as my eyes and ears in the bureau, these women were very important advisors to me and to their bosses about personnel matters affecting navy women. Another officer and a woman chief did the same for enlisted women.

I made arrangements to give a collateral fitness report to the division head for the navy women working in each of these key divisions. In this way, I was holding them responsible for plans and programs essential to the development, assignment, and promotion of navy women. My authority to issue the fitness reports assured them that they would receive the recognition and credit they needed from their work with me. My fitness report on them also advised their bosses of the work they had done for me.

Women officers were selected to the next higher rank by promotion boards, which usually consisted of a senior captain and six to nine other senior male officers and one senior woman officer. The expansion of career opportunities for women was a gradual process that depended upon an internal public relations program designed to keep the navy aware of the increasing talents of its female personnel. But it was always an uphill battle to get the first woman accepted in a new technical assignment. Once she performed her duties in an outstanding manner, the problem disappeared, paving the way for another woman officer's easy acceptance. The same was true for enlisted women in key jobs.

It was clear to me from the beginning of my new assignment that central to career advancement for women in the navy, as for men, was the opportunity for continuous education in new fields. If a woman officer or enlisted woman could not enroll in an educational program, her career could not advance in any area where special technical training was required. I found that women were not being given the opportunity for many educational programs—

both within the navy and outside—not because they were unqualified professionally, but simply because they were were not men. At the very top educational level, women could not enter the Naval Academy, since admission there required a change in the law, a change that did not take place until 1976—fourteen years after I retired from the navy. My efforts were aimed at having women officers *teach* at the Naval Academy, since no law prevented that option and they were teaching at many other naval schools.[8] Furthermore, there were many women officers highly qualified in science and mathematics—important subjects in the educational curriculum at the Naval Academy.

My boss at this time was Vice Admiral W. R. Smedberg III, a very fine officer who nevertheless did not agree with me. He said, "It wouldn't be acceptable to have women instructors at the Naval Academy. The superintendent would never accept midshipmen being taught by a woman naval officer instead of a man."

"Men have been taught by women all their lives," I replied. "I don't see any difference just because it's the Naval Academy."

Although he was supportive of me in most of my requests, he never agreed with me on this one. It was not until 1972 that women became instructors at the Naval Academy. Women had been teaching navy men and women in the navy's technical schools going back to World War II. It took persuasion to get the first woman in a teaching post at a graduate navy school such as the Naval War College. Normally, as a first step, women were admitted as students in those navy graduate schools. Once this precedent was established, then other women were accepted as instructors or retained on staff assignments.

In 1957, I found a particularly egregious situation of gender discrimination as it relates to educational opportunity. I learned that enlisted men *without* a baccalaureate degree (and often without a high school degree) were being selected for an officer's commission as ensigns, based strictly on past performance, competitive examination, and a selection board recommendation. No enlisted women were being selected despite the fact that all of our enlisted women had the equivalent of a high school education and some had some college educational experience and even college degrees. I arranged for a meeting with the assistant chief of naval personnel for plans, an admiral, who had to approve this program. I explained the quality of our enlisted women and asked him why they were not eligible. He said, "I am opposed because you would be diluting the quality of your officer corps."

"Admiral, you know perfectly well that navy women are not a separate corps," I replied. "With minor exceptions, there are no separate billets for either women officers or enlisted personnel. Women are an integrated part of the navy and the enlisted women are much better educated than the enlisted men you are selecting for officers. I want my enlisted women to have this opportunity to become commissioned."

When my plea did not convince him, I continued: "I feel you have no rational reason for not approving my request. If you still refuse to accept the enlisted women for this program, I intend to go to the chief of the Bureau of Naval Personnel and I hope you will go with me."

He still refused, but he did agree to join me in the meeting. He shared his reasoning with the chief: "She is trying to dilute her

wonderful officer corps by letting enlisted women become officers."

"What do you say to that?" the chief asked me.

"Admiral Smedberg, I have brought you three fitness jackets
of three enlisted women whom I feel are far better educated than
the male enlistees who are being commissioned."

Admiral Smedberg looked over the fitness files of these chiefs.
One woman had a B.A. and the two others had some college education. All three had excellent records of past performance.

"I think these are wonderfully educated young women and
they should certainly have an opportunity to be commissioned,"
the chief said. "As of this meeting, I not only approve these three
but I recommend all qualified enlisted women have the same opportunities for commissions as enlisted men."

The assistant chief for plans accepted Admiral Smedberg's
decision without further discussion. The first enlisted woman selected, Chief Mary Driver, was commissioned a lieutenant (jg) in
1958.

Sometimes, denying educational opportunities to women was
a matter of oversight rather than conscious discrimination, since
there were so few women in the navy in comparison with the
large number of men. While I recognized that navy plans had been
designed by and for men, it was my job to go to the policymakers
and present a woman officer candidate, highly qualified, to be
approved for admission to key educational programs such as the
War College. All the top naval male officers who attended the
War College and made top grades found that prestigious assign-

ments had opened for them. There was no reason that a woman couldn't qualify for this advanced education.

In 1957, Lieutenant Commander Jane Potter became the first woman staff member of the Naval War College. She concurrently attended the intermediate course, which all staff members are privileged to do during their three-year tour. Vice Admiral Stuart H. Ingersoll, college president at the time, reluctantly accepted a woman officer as a staff member. Upon completion of the intermediate course, Ingersoll welcomed women officers. Potter's performance had been so outstanding that he no longer had any prejudice about accepting women officers as students and staff members. Lieutenant Commander Potter's next assignment was at the new Amphibious School in Norfolk, where she was the head of the department working on planned fleet amphibious exercises.

Once that initial barrier was eliminated, the rest was easy. A precedent had been established, and other women followed—first as students and later as instructors and staff officers. Between 1964 and 1974, eight women were assigned as students at the Naval War College. By 1975, women officers were routinely ordered into the Naval War College as students in both the senior and the intermediate courses.

Women moved not only into new educational programs but into new assignments as well. Some of the new and more responsible assignments for women officers were on the staffs of senior commanders and on shore-based fleet commands. I was continuously opening opportunities for enlisted women to receive commissions as officers. At my request the chief of naval personnel wrote to the navy JAG requesting that enlisted women be approved for appointment as regular officers of the navy designated for limited duty (LDO). In January 1961, the navy JAG approved of this change, which was a real achievement in enlisted women's opportunity for a commission.

While I was in my top navy post, enlisted navy women were assigned as aerographers, air controlmen, storekeepers, photographers, yeomen, radiomen, communications technicians, personnel men, machine accountants, disbursing clerks, journalists, hospital and dental technicians, electronic technicians, draftsmen, opticalmen, lithographers, instruments men, data technicians, X-ray technicians, link trainers, and in some of the new jet and seagoing nuclear positions. New scientific developments involved a technological revolution within the navy, the most significant component of which was the employment of jet-powered airplanes and nuclear-powered ships. Each of these fields required new skills and new training programs. Opportunities in both aviation and the nuclear program required enlisted personnel in the existing ratings, such as electronic technicians, radiomen, and technicians (including communications technicians), but their duties were very different and required additional training. Women became a part of this expansion because of a shortage of males with relevant technical skills.

The push toward moving women into new technical areas was hastened not only by the rapid development of technology itself, but by the Korean War, which necessitated a rapid expansion of navy personnel, mostly from the reserves. Many of these reservists—including women officers and enlisted women—were not discharged when the war ended, but continued on active duty for a full navy career.

---

[1] The person who assigns personnel to a duty station.

[2] He had earned his nickname in the Pacific in World War II when his destroyer surpassed its designed speed limit.

[3] Also, the late 1950s was a period in which the navy as a whole was confronted with low morale and low quality in recruiting, as a result of public apathy toward the military.

[4] In the 1970s and 1980s, civilian women used the term *glass ceiling* to describe the insurmountable barriers that prevented them from rising to leadership positions within an organization.

[5] Captain Louise Wilde files, 1953–1957.

[6] The law did not change until 1967—five years after I retired. The 1967 law (Public Law 90-130) removed the cap on the numbers of military women, allowed women to compete for promotion through the grade of captain/colonel, and enabled appointment of women flag and general officers. This law produced a dynamic change in equal opportunity for military women. When the military moved away from the draft to an all-volunteer force in the 1970s, women achieved even more opportunities because of the reluctance of some men to serve in the armed forces.

[7] The school for women had been established in Newport in December 1948 with a class of twenty-nine prospective officers. Lieutenant Sybil Grant was the officer in charge in 1948. In 1957, the school had eight women instructors. This school was a separate school for women but was part of the Indoctrination School Command. It had bachelors officers' quarters and mess facilities available for both men and women.

[8] The Naval Academy is at college level. Candidates—men and women—must pass an entrance examination, have a high academic record, as well as leadership and athletic activity in high school. Investigation must reveal individuals of high moral character and excellent reputation. In addition, the candidates must be recommended by a congressman or senator. Upon graduation, they receive a bachelor's degree and are commissioned as ensigns. Women were admitted to the three military academies in 1976.

Graduate education for naval officers is continuous as well as constantly changing with new scientific and technical developments. The postgraduate school at Monterey offers courses of fifteen to thirty months. A graduate degree is awarded upon successful completion. A wide range of technical and nontechnical subjects is available, including aerological and aeronautical engineering, air combat intelligence, air operation, air navigation, nuclear engineering, submarine training, language, naval architecture, operation analysis, atomic chemistry, and personnel management. Currently, there are 500 U.S. officers plus some foreign officers in the Monterey program.

The Naval War College in Newport gives two training programs for intermediate and senior officers. The intermediate program is for lieutenant commanders and commanders. The senior program is for navy captains, and marine, army, air force, and foreign officers of equivalent rank. The courses emphasize the strategic planning in sea and air naval warfare. The senior courses emphasize war planning at command level

Schools for enlisted personnel must match many of the technical and nontechnical subjects that are taught in schools for officers. These courses include antiaircraft training, mine-warfare training, submarine chaser training, mine sweepers, yeomen, gunners' mates, fire control, and nuclear training.

six

REMOVING ROADBLOCKS FOR NAVY WOMEN

In addition to working within the navy system to improve the status of women officers and enlisted women, I also initiated programs designed to educate civilians about the possibilities of military life for women. I felt that, with a good public relations program designed to call attention to the expanded career opportunities, we could win civilian support, attract gifted young women to our programs, and improve morale among women who were already in military service. I specifically wanted to call attention to the new opportunities in the navy arising from the technological revolution in the nuclear age.

I made it a point to attend national conferences of the deans of women at colleges and universities. I often gave formal speeches at these occasions, which gave me a great opportunity to discuss what women in the navy were doing. By citing job assignments and advanced education, I stressed that in most cases, navy women were being given greater opportunities than women could find in civilian society. When I mentioned the fact that we were taking only one out of ten female officer applicants, and one out of five female enlisted applicants, the deans knew that women who got into the navy had to be eminently qualified. I stressed that we were only taking high-quality, educated women—and the message finally got through.

The deans always asked questions about the kinds of jobs navy women held, about promotion and retirement opportunities, and about living conditions. Meeting with them gave me a chance to correct many misconceptions. Because I understood that the chances of a positive reaction to a woman recruiter would be enhanced by her appearance, speaking ability, and personality, I made sure that we assigned the most attractive, articulate, and motivated women officers and enlisted petty officers for recruiting duty. This duty was equivalent to sea duty for men and enhanced the women's promotion opportunities. I also solicited qualified women naval reservists to give talks to college groups and to women and men's professional and civic organizations. Enlisted recruiters visited high schools and officer recruiters visited colleges to give talks on opportunities in the navy.

Through all of these efforts, we began to get improvement in the numbers and quality of women applying for a commission and enlistment. But I wanted to do even more. As an experiment, I initiated a letter to the parents of each daughter who had been an outstanding recruit or a top graduate of our officer candidates school, asking them if they would share their responses to the navy's program for their daughters. Here is the letter I sent:

Dear _____:

Your daughter's record has come to my attention, and I wish to commend you on her achievement. She is an outstanding young woman and I am sure you share with me a great deal of pride in her accomplishments.

Now that you have had an opportunity to know the details of her navy life, I would be most interested in hearing your comments and suggestions. Many parents have asked me questions about the supervision and the moral and spiritual guidance given navy women both in their work and living situations. Some parents feel concern about the kinds of young people their daughter will meet when she leaves home for the first time and joins such a vast organization as the U.S. Navy. Others are interested in their daughter's chance for advancement, and the salary, promotional, educational opportunities and retirement. They are concerned about the living conditions and medical care available to their daughter.

These are serious questions and I can well understand a parent's concern. I am also sure that you had many similar questions and it is for this reason that I am writing to you.

We wish to attract only the finest young American women to join the U.S. Navy. In order to do this, we must answer parents' questions about navy life and thereby, I hope, convince them that their daughter may have the same opportunity and supervision as yours has received.

Your thoughts on this matter would be most helpful to me and I know would mean so much to other parents. If at your convenience, you would write to me giving me this most helpful information, it would certainly be appreciated.

Kindest personal regards and best wishes for your daughter's continued success.

All of their replies were positive, as the following excerpts from some of the letters indicate:

Our daughter told us that the navy women's living quarters are well supervised and that the girls themselves are given constant guidance, particularly during the first few months they are on active duty with the navy.

I think that my daughter has gained a lot in the way of poise, self-assurance, and satisfaction with her work in the naval service. I know that she is happy and this relieves me of any anxiety concerning her.

I only wish I could talk to the parents who have doubts about their daughter's joining the naval service. I have met many of the young women my daughter has served with. They are all fine people with high moral standards, and all seem very proud to be representing their country. Their enthusiasm is wonderful.

My daughter spent three years stationed in London. She saw almost all of Europe. While there she completed two years of her college education. The University of Maryland offers a home study course for service personnel, so she is now working on her third year. Besides these advantages, she has attended some of the navy's service schools which have improved her in her line of work. This will be of great benefit to her if she ever decides to return to civilian life.

As parents, we naturally were concerned about our daughter's leaving home for the first time. And she is now a long distance from home. However, with the medical care, religious, social, and educational facilities available to her through the naval service, we are delighted over her well-being. It has given her an outstanding opportunity.

After receiving the parents' letters, I wrote letters to the daughters' high school principals or college presidents, enclosing the parents' enthusiastic responses. This correspondence opened doors for recruiters at both high schools and colleges and helped to improve the image of the navy and to educate teachers about the high caliber of young women being accepted. As a high school teacher of a recent recruit training graduate commented: "I wish to commend most highly the training that has given this girl so much poise, confidence, and a real love for the navy. I have known her for the past five years and am delighted at the splendid improvement she has made in so short a time."

In order to broaden our public relations efforts, I participated in naval activities in the United States and abroad, where I had the advantage of press exposure in newspapers, radio, and television. I also sent out a directive to all officers and senior petty officers that their participation in speaking engagements in high schools, colleges, and civic and professional groups would be looked upon very positively when promotion decisions were made.

I assigned an attractive, bright, and articulate woman, Lieutenant Julia Brown, to the staff of the inspector of recruiting. Her job was twofold: (1) to evaluate the efforts and success made at

Captain Collins being interviewed on CBS, on the occasion of the WAVES nineteenth anniversary in 1961. Official photograph of the Office of Secretary of the Air Force.

each recruiting station in terms of methods used in attracting women and (2) with the help of navy public relations and the National Navy League, to speak to civic and educational groups, and to give television, radio, and press interviews to discuss opportunities for navy women. In her reports, she told me that at many recruiting offices, navy males were discouraging women from joining the navy—implying that it wasn't a place for women. When she gave me the names of specific individuals, I went to their boss and said, "This is what's happening." And it was happening too often. The admiral who was in charge of the recruiting command sent out a directive to recruiting stations prohibiting any negative messages about navy women. The admiral said to me, "It won't happen anymore with male recruiters." And as far as I know, it didn't.

Happily these efforts paid off, and publicity on women in the navy vastly improved with wider dissemination of radio and television clips, recruiting posters, informational brochures, and syndicated articles on duty assignments, travel experiences, and accomplishments of navy women. The quality of our recruits was increased and the interest of educational counselors and parents was heightened. We also saw an increase in the number of recruits. When I first became captain in 1957, there were 295 female regular navy line officers and 261 reserve line officers on active duty. We had 100 staff line officers plus 96 U.S. naval reserve officers on active duty. By the time of my retirement in 1962, we had 345 line officers with 61 line ensigns (with a large number in the Women's Officer Indoctrination School) and 129 active duty reservists, 1,590 active staff officers, and 1,196 reservists on active duty plus 5,847 active enlisted personnel (including 11 women warrant officers).[1] The figure of 406 active duty regular navy women officers was the highest number attained since 1948. Since promotion of women officers was based solely on the number of active duty women officers, the increase in numbers greatly enhanced promotion opportunities over the years.

HOW YOU CAN HELP TO HASTEN VICTORY

•

Today, with the stepped-up tempo of naval action in the Pacific, more *WAVES* are still needed for the important Navy jobs that must be done before final victory. *WAVES* are wanted for radio, aviation, hospital, communications, administrative, and clerical work. Every job done by a *WAVE* helps bring the day of victory nearer.

Members of the *Women's Reserve* have won admiration and respect from Navy men — praise and honor from their communities, their families, their friends.

The *WAVES* uphold the highest traditions of the Navy; they increase the efficiency of the Navy afloat by taking their places ashore in the execution of essential work.

Read this booklet carefully. It will help you picture your life as a *Navy WAVE* — and to make up your mind that, in wartime, this is the place where you belong.

James Forrestal

Secretary of the Navy

Front of a U.S. Navy recruiting booklet, 1943.

⚓ ⚓ ⚓

The anniversary of the legislation establishing the WAVES on July 30, 1942, often provided an opportunity to further the public relations program for navy women, serving as a means of sharing stories, pictures, and television and radio interviews. It linked our goals more closely to the navy, the other services, and political and cultural leaders. It necessitated my being featured in many press conferences to discuss details of the life of navy women, their education, their jobs, and other matters, and it gave other navy women on active duty and in the reserves an opportunity to participate in press activities. I always asked the chief of naval personnel, the secretary of the navy, and other high-ranking officers to send greetings to the navy women on each anniversary. It was reassuring to read their glowing remarks of our accomplishments and it helped me set new goals. The comments of the navy leaders, emphasizing the contributions of navy women, reached the naval personnel and the public. This helped the morale and the pride of navy women.

WAVES sixteenth birthday celebration on board U.S. carrier *Franklin D. Roosevelt*, 6 August 1958. Left to right, back row: U. O'Toole, YNC; P. Vick, SN; four unidentified women from USNH St. Albans. Middle row: L. Moriconi, YN2; LTJG Jane Osborne; ENS Leonides Garcia-Martinez; F. Perrell, TE1; LCDR Dorothy Francis; M. Myers, YNC; L. Jodoin, DKSN. Front row: Rear Admiral Chester C. Wood, Commandant 3ND; Captain Collins. Official U.S. Navy photograph.

Captain Collins arrives at Los Angeles airport to celebrate the nineteenth anniversary of the WAVES. Left to right: Lieutenant Jeanne Hoeck, Captain Collins, LCDR Lois Wilson. In front is the "junior" WAVE Karen Woolley. August 1961. Official Photo USAF.

Captain Collins with Ronald Reagan, master of ceremonies for the WAVES nineteenth birthday celebration. Official photo USAF.

In 1960, a ceremony for the eighteenth anniversary of the WAVES was held in Dallas, Texas, where the navy women were to honor the international designer of women's fashion, Main Rousseau Bocher, who had designed the navy women's uniform in World War II. At the banquet, I had the pleasure of presenting to him the navy's Meritorious Public Service Award, the only time in the history of the navy that it was given to an individual in the fashion industry. In his response, he said, "Among my famous customers are Helen Hayes, Mary Martin, the Duchess of Windsor, and the United States Navy WAVES. The WAVES are one of my dearest treasures. I am thrilled to share this occasion with you in accepting this very high award from the secretary of the navy."

⚓ ⚓ ⚓

During my tenure as captain, the performance and the conduct of women in the navy were first rate. Reports from commanding officers reflected what I saw on my inspection trips: morale was good, and there were very few discipline cases. Every month in the weekly staff meetings conducted by the chief of naval personnel, the assistant chiefs would review all the discipline cases. I would listen to reports on men in navy prisons accused of rape, murder, disorderly conduct, drunkenness, etc. When it came my turn to speak, I could always say, "For navy women, I don't have a single case of rape, murder, assault, battery, disorderly conduct, or drunkenness." I do not recall any instance in which a navy woman was put in the brig, although they were subject to the same discipline regulations as were the men. I did have to report pregnancies, because at that time, pregnant women were automatically discharged from the service.[2]

Although I was aware of some of the harassment suffered by navy women, I did not deal directly with the offenders. When cases came to my attention, I would go to the commanding officer in charge of the accused and say, "This is what your enlisted men (or your officers) are reportedly doing." I found that harassment was mostly a problem for enlisted women rather than women officers, and I thought the reason was that the enlisted men had no experience, in either civilian or military life, with competent, educated women. Harrassment—particularly in the area of demeaning remarks—was the men's way of exerting power over them. Worse yet, there were incidents of fondling or rape, but these matters were handled by commanding officers and the legal department, although the former often consulted me for advice. Commanding officers and senior petty officers—both men and women—did a fine job in monitoring such incidents.

Even the navy women not subject to harrassment had problems of acceptance by their male colleagues. An individual woman—enlisted or officer—had to prove herself on a one-to-one basis with her boss and her coworkers. Many navy men, like men in civilian life, readily accepted any notion about navy women that would reinforce their preconceived idea that women weren't as important, as intelligent, or as competent, as men.

One frequent charge the men made was that the navy invests too much time and money in women, who in turn leave for a civilian life at a higher rate than men do. I had heard this charge made so many times that I decided to investigate. I made a study of the number of men discharged from the navy for various reasons and found the rate of dishonorable discharge for males to be quite high, mostly because of discipline problems. Women did have a slightly higher discharge rate, but it was mostly due to pregnancy or marriage.

I turned my attention to *whom* navy women were marrying and learned that in most cases it was navy men. The next time I heard criticism at a staff meeting, I responded: "The navy is getting a double benefit when a navy woman marries a navy man, since she knows a great deal about the navy and can be a far more supportive wife than if she lacked navy experience." I also said that even when women left the navy, they still served American society. As Admiral Arleigh Burke used to say, the navy exists to serve society, and one way to serve it is to train people to do better once they get to civilian life. Navy women received magnificent training in a three-year, four-year, or six-year period. Because they went to advanced schools in the navy, they were hired immediately by industry because of their superb qualifications. True, when the men or women left, replacing them was expensive to the navy. But it was not a loss to the nation; it was a gain.

One problem that faced many career navy women was how to adjust their careers when they got married, the same kind of problem that many civilian couples face when both husband and wife are in the work force. In the military, there is an additional burden: separation is inevitable. The navy did not want to lose superior talent by making life difficult for navy women and men who chose to marry, so it made an effort to keep married couples in the same geographical areas where possible. Beginning in 1961, a married navy woman could request assignment with her navy spouse and vice versa. That policy change was a great morale booster, since in the old system, no special attempts were made to keep a family unit together—even if it were possible to do so. Of course, under both the old and the new policy, when a man went to sea, there was no way that the navy could have the woman go to sea with him. Navy women accepted their husbands' requirements of sea duty but they were delighted that the prospects of staying together as a family unit were enhanced by the new policy.

⚓ ⚓ ⚓

Soon after I became a captain, I was shocked to learn that the public perception of navy women was that they were unfeminine. I recognized that navy women's physical appearance was important both in terms of self-esteem (it could benefit their morale), and in terms of influencing civilian women who might be encouraged to join the navy. Previous regulations, such as those requiring women to have short hair cuts and wear black shoes with low or flat heels, needed to be changed if the perception of navy women was to change.

In January 1961, I told our enlisted women and our officers, "I do not want to see a single mannish haircut. Longer hair makes you look more attractive. We women are here because the navy wants *women* in the navy—not women looking like men." The rule up to that time was that if hair fell below the bottom of a woman's collar, it was too long. I changed the rule to allow for longer and more feminine hairstyles, and organized a grooming and self-improvement program in which, with the help of a woman chief in each of the enlisted barracks, I was able to get a beautician to volunteer her time and give individual suggestions at every station. The beauticians were eager to volunteer and enjoyed doing this to help navy women. I wrote each beautician a letter complimenting her on her patriotic volunteer service.

Another problem related to the public perception of navy women as unfeminine was what I felt was an unrealistic weight requirement for navy women. The Bureau of Medicine's weight standard was ten pounds heavier than any of the national insurance requirements. I was unable to insist on a woman losing weight with our navy weight requirements so high. I discussed this problem with the doctor (a captain) who was responsible for weight standards of navy personnel, but he continued to be opposed to lowering the weight standards. I finally gave up on him and went to the admiral of the Bureau of Medicine and Surgery, who readily agreed with me.

The irate physician captain called me and said, "I hope you're satisfied to have all your women coming in as bean poles!"

"I'm delighted," I replied. "Don't worry; we can always add a little padding here and there!"

We also had in our regulations a requirement that hosiery had to have seams, heels had to be low, and skirt lengths long. These were just a few of the old-fashioned dress regulations that navy women had to follow. I made it permissible for navy women to wear seamless hosiery, changed the shoe standards so that heels on pumps could be raised a half-inch from what they had been, and allowed skirt length rules to comply with current civilian fashion. I thought that these changes were more attractive and more feminine. So did the navy women!

I designed or arranged for some other changes in uniforms. For instance, I was able to obtain approval for a white plastic hat top, replacing the linen hat that was difficult to keep clean. The plastic looked just like linen and all we had to do to clean it was just wipe it off. Also, I designed a pair of dacron slacks that looked much more feminine than the dungarees that some navy women— such as aircraft mechanics—had to wear for their jobs. I also tackled the job of redesigning the existing summer uniform, which had been a navy standard since World War II. Made of gray striped cotton seersucker, the summer uniform looked more like a maid's housedress than a military uniform. I wanted a new one that would look smart, be easy to care for, and meet the requirements of navy women wherever they were stationed around the world. I worked with the head of a commercial firm and designed what I thought would be ideal. A field test in warm climates revealed that navy women were greatly in favor of the new uniform. But it had to be approved by the all-male Uniform Board. I decided that having an attractive young enlisted woman wear the new uniform and a not-quite-so-attractive one wearing the old one would assure my getting approval. Two hours before the meeting, however, I was told that my model for the new uniform was ill. I scrambled to find a substitute, but the petty officer replacement did not measure up to the attractiveness of the preselected woman, so I decided to rely exclusively on facts.

"The new uniform will cost the same as the ugly 'mattress material' uniform. Also, all the navy women I quizzed find the new uniform attractive and easy to care for," I said.

The senior admiral, who was extremely dogmatic, said: "I like the old one. I can't understand why you want a new one. I think the young lady in that gray looks very attractive." He was not interested in the facts I presented about how the navy women liked the new uniform, how easily it could be laundered, and how it could be worn in all climates and used everywhere a navy woman was stationed throughout the world.

Luckily, a captain in the supply corps who was responsible for materials procurement spoke up at that moment and said, "Admiral, we have yards and yards of that gray seersucker material on the shelves, but it's rotting. In terms of cost, it will be the same price to replace the gray material as it will be to buy the new blue material."

When the summer uniform of the WAVES made its Great Lakes debut, two Naval Examining Center WAVES were among the first to sport the trim ensemble. Gordon Gilbertson, YN3, glances in approval at Ann Bennett, SN (left) and Pat Sullivan, MA3. Official U.S. Navy photograph.

The admiral reluctantly agreed and approved the new uniform. Later I gave that supply corps captain a heartfelt thanks, as his statement had turned the tide. The new summer uniform was approved in late 1957, but it took a year to get sufficient supplies to all the navy women.

I also proposed a uniform change for female chief petty officers, who wanted to wear the same dark blue color worn by male chief petty officers rather than the lighter shade of blue they had at the time. After much discussion with the Uniform Board, which was always resistant to any suggested changes, the new uniform was approved for the enlisted petty officers with no additional cost to the navy. At one naval station shortly after the approval went through, I was addressing the women senior petty officers. One of the chiefs said she thought the navy should have to pay for the new uniforms. I was annoyed with her complaint, as I had worked very hard to get this change past the board.

"Weren't you one of those who was so desirous to have this change?" I asked.

"Yes."

"Do you have an automobile and if so what is its model and year?" I asked.

She told me that she had the latest model of an expensive car.

"I'll tell you how you pay for your new uniform," I said. "You reach down in the same pocket that paid for your automobile and take out the money to pay for the new uniform. And I don't want to hear any further complaint from you." The other senior petty officers laughed and applauded me.

In 1960, I received approval for the adoption of a new full-dress summer uniform in synthetic material (Arnel) for the women officers and chief petty officers. The previous material varied in "whiteness" from a cream to a pinkish color, a difference both discernible and unattractive when seen in a group of women. In consultation with two manufacturers of tailor-made women's uniforms, I created the new formal uniform, a tailored blue-black mohair with a navy gold-buttoned short mess jacket worn over a white ruffled front dress shirt with a black band under the collar. The latter style was suggestive of the naval tradition of a tie. The six-gored skirt, available in a short and a long length, was slightly flared with a left side slit, and a gold cummerbund. Rank was indicated by gold braid on the jacket sleeves with the corps insignia in gold embroidery above the gold stripes. An optional black velvet tiara was embroidered in gold and silver officer insignia. Accessories included a black evening bag, 2-1/2 inch heeled pumps, seamless hosiery, and white gloves. The formal uniform could also be tailored in white tropical worsted with white accessories (with the same tiara optional).

The secretary of the navy approved the new uniform early in 1962. *Women's Wear*, a fashion magazine for civilian women, called it "an imaginative design of navy tradition and femininity." The Wool Makers Association invited me to New York for a special dinner at which actress Celeste Holm presented me with their "Golden Fleece" award for the creativity of the design. The other women's services—army, air force, and marines—later adopted a similar design for their women officers.

I first unveiled the new navy women's evening dress at a formal Navy League affair in Washington, D.C., and it met with the approval of both military and civilians. It is still worn today. When I ask navy women officers if they like it, they respond with enthusiasm. The new uniform has been a boost to morale.

Improved morale was also a consequence of women's involvement in a navy leadership program. Like other high-ranking navy officers, I understood the importance of recognizing and developing leadership qualities. In 1960, when the chief of naval operations established a navy-wide leadership program to reemphasize the importance of leadership techniques for officers, petty officers and senior-ranked enlisted personnel, I wanted

Captain Winifred Quick Collins, USN, unveils the new WAVE evening dress as she chats with the Naval Aide to the President, Captain Tazewell T. Shepard, Jr., USN (on the left), and Thomas A. Callaghan, Jr., President, District of Columbia Council (on the right), 1961. Official U.S. Navy photograph.

to make certain that women were included. I started a pilot pro-gram for women consisting of a series of discussions directed at the psychological aspects of navy women petty officers and women officer leadership. Our purpose was to more closely define the role of women in the navy and clarify the different roles of men and women. On a trial basis these discussions were presented in the Washington area for fifteen hours over a two-week period to all women officers and enlisted senior ratings. The results showed a need to develop unity among personnel, self-esteeem and pride in being a woman, and responsibility to others in the navy and civilian community.

Based on these findings, leadership teams were trained to visit all naval activities ashore and at sea. Two teams of women were trained to visit activities where women were stationed. The team accompanying me on my inspection trips helped tremendously to instill pride in being a navy woman. The progress of the leader-ship program was a continuous item of discussion at my weekly staff conferences with the chief of naval personnel, and I gave it rave reviews.

As part of the program, I developed a community relations policy in which officers and enlisted personnel volunteered to par-ticipate in activities such as visits to children's hospitals or senior citizen homes or assistance to YWCA programs. They also raised money to send underprivileged children to summer camps. These kinds of activities were especially beneficial to the younger en-listed women, adding greatly to the public's image of the high caliber of navy women.

⚓ ⚓ ⚓

Although I worked hard in my post as assistant chief, the job was not without its advantages. I was an invited guest to many formal and informal events at which I was able to meet famous people. One occasion was particularly special for me. In the fall of 1957, I received an invitation from the British ambassador to a reception at the British Embassy in Washington, D.C., in honor of Queen Elizabeth and her husband, Prince Philip, who were making a state visit to the United States. Senior U.S. Navy officers were there, and I was thrilled to be invited to the reception. Both the Queen and Prince Philip were impressed with my navy uniform. The Prince was even staring at it. "That is smashing," he said. It was an exciting time for me.

Although I often met top navy people as a direct consequence of my job, I also met them occasionally in the most unanticipated manner. One of the strangest of such meetings was with Admiral Hyman Rickover, the man who did so much in the development of nuclear submarines. The particular subject which brought us together was not some matter of national security but rather a food article in which I was featured.

The food editor of the *Washington Star*, Violet Faulkner, on hearing that I enjoyed cooking, asked me if I would do an article for her newspaper. I was excited about the prospect and decided I would have a Chinese dinner called "Winnie Wong's Recipes." The day after the article appeared in the Sunday edition of the *Washington Star*, I received a call from Admiral Rickover. He said, "I want to congratulate you on that interesting article about your cooking talents. I think it is wonderful publicity for the navy, especially its women."

I thanked the admiral but told him I hadn't been thinking of the article as good navy publicity, just a lot of fun to do. A few days later he called and asked me for a favor. "I'm going to Russia in the next few days," he said. "I wonder if you would bake me a cake for Nikita Khrushchev[3] and put some arsenic in it."

"I'm sorry, admiral," I said. "But I don't bake cakes because sweets aren't good nutrition."

He laughed and I asked him if he would give me a call when he came back and tell me about his trip. He did, and spent an hour telling me about his fascinating Russian experiences. I had constant contact with him after the cooking incident, since he wanted navy women in his nuclear program. He personally interviewed and selected the personnel for his program, because he wanted only the top intellectual navy men and women, officers and enlisted personnel, for his program.

In his interviews, as he was evaluating the individual, he asked a lot of intimate questions about the candidates' sexual habits. I thought these were totally inappropriate, and I repeatedly expressed my view to him on this subject. I always spoke with each woman before she was interviewed for the nuclear program and warned her that the admiral was going to ask her some very personal questions. I advised her that if she did not wish to answer them or did not want to work for him because of the questions, it would in no way have a negative effect on her career as I was the one in charge of her career, not the admiral.

One very bright lieutenant (jg) had been selected by the admiral for an interview, so I talked to her beforehand and warned her about his questions. In the course of the interview, when he asked the intimate questions, she said, "Admiral, Captain Quick said I didn't have to answer your questions on this subject as she felt they were inappropriate. And I am not going to answer them."

Immediately I received a call from the admiral, who asked me if she was quoting me correctly.

"Yes," I said. "And Admiral, as you know, I have discussed this matter with you many times and do not approve of what you are asking women personnel."

"She's terrific," he responded. "I want her on my staff."

My opinion is that Admiral Rickover admired individuals who stood up to him. He always treated me very courteously, but I also always made my point of view clear. He was an acknowledged expert in the nuclear program for submarines and ships. He gave the impression, however, that he was an expert in many fields having nothing to do with the navy and consistently expressed his views on these subjects. I saw evidence of this when my deputy, Commander Viola Sanders, and I were invited to Boston for the launching of a new nuclear frigate which Admiral Rickover had designed. Commander Sanders and I were wearing our new summer uniforms which I had designed. She went over to greet the admiral and said, "Sir, this is our new summer uniform."

"I don't like it," he replied. This was a typical answer of Admiral Rickover. Early Monday morning, he called me to express his opinion again: "I don't like your new uniform."

"Admiral, I am very disappointed that you don't like it, because I worked for a year on the design," I said. "It has been tested by many women and it has met the easy-care requirements of navy women around the world. They all find it very attractive and are eager to have it available to them. On the other hand, Admiral, I don't know a darned thing about submarines."

"Message understood," he said and hung up.

After I had retired, I met him at a cocktail party, which was a rare event because he hardly ever attended such social gatherings. When I went up to say hello, he asked me, "Did I ever give you a rug?"

"If so, I have no recollection of it," I said.

"I'll send you one tomorrow."

I called his aide, who turned out to be a woman officer, to inquire about this "gift." She said, "Captain, I hope you understand my position. All I can say is that you will be surprised." The next morning a driver in a sedan arrived. He needed my signature to prove I had personally received his gift, so I had to go to our gatehouse. The "gift" turned out to be a piece of linoleum, printed with the words: "QUICK'S RUG." It fit inside my grocery cart.

I didn't call the Admiral to thank him for what was, in my opinion, a ridiculous gift! He was a very strange, intelligent, and politically powerful person.

⚓ ⚓ ⚓

Like other people in high-level government posts, I looked for help wherever I could find it, often in the navy community itself.

Fortunately, I always had a close relationship with the wives of the secretaries of the navy. Mrs. William Franke, for instance, was a very special friend. She invited me to lunch one day and asked if she could be of any help concerning navy women when her husband made visits to navy establishments. She also asked if it would be possible for me to accompany the secretary on these trips because accompanying the top leader of the navy would be looked upon as being a prestigious role for me. I answered that I would very much like to join the secretary's party whenever it was possible, but meanwhile her assistance would be wonderful. I outlined a list of suggested activities for her, including inspection of enlisted women's barracks and facilities (e.g., washing machines, refrigerators, stoves, hair dryers, and recreational activities available for women). Also, I felt it would be a morale builder for navy women if she could talk with them informally to discover major problems they were having.

Mrs. Franke was a tremendous help in assisting me to get better equipment for living quarters and recreational facilities for the enlisted women. She was a charming and diplomatic lady. She asked the enlisted women questions on the things I suggested that they needed and they responded with enthusiasm and frankness. She made the enlisted women feel important because she was personally interested in them. The commanding officers were, of course, very responsive to her suggestions, passed along to them through the woman officer who accompanied her.

In addition to finding help within the navy, I also relied on other sources such as the Defense Advisory Committee on Women in the Services (DACOWITS), which had been created in July 1951.

The committee consisted of fifty women from all parts of the country selected on the basis of their achievements in various professions as well as in community leadership. They were appointed for two-year terms. These intelligent people were increasingly helpful in solving some of the problems of women in the military. At each biannual meeting, they would visit one of the military installations where military women were assigned. They were also a tremendous help to the women military leaders in making recommendations to the secretary of defense regarding policy and legislative matters. It was through the efforts of DACOWITS, under the chairmanship of Mrs. Donald A. Quarles, that in the fall of 1961 the matter of statutory restriction on the numbers of women officers in the various grades was brought to the attention of a president's commission, which reviewed the laws and policies governing women of the armed services. The subsequent enactment of legislation eliminating legal limits on the number of women officers marked a very significant step forward for women in the armed services.

⚓ ⚓ ⚓

Like everyone else in the navy, I had both a professional and a personal life to live. Sometimes, however, the two lives crossed. Captain Howard Collins, whom I had met at Admiral Nimitz's quarters at a luncheon when I arrived at Pearl Harbor in 1944, went to sea shortly after I had met him. At sea, he was the commander of Destroyer Squadron Ten, consisting of twelve new destroyers operating with a carrier task force off the coast of Japan. The ships under his command remained with the occupation forces in Japan until 1946. Following this assignment, he became commanding officer of the U.S.S. *Helena*, and then, in 1953, commanding officer of the Military Sea Transportation Service, Pacific, where he was responsible for ocean transportation, ashore and afloat, of personnel and cargo with operations in San Francisco, Seattle, Guam, Honolulu, Anchorage, and Long Beach. Under his command were fifty tankers and 6,000 personnel. His headquarters were in San Francisco, where I was serving as director of naval personnel at the time. When our paths crossed again, I met his attractive wife Peggy, and thereafter saw them on many official and informal social occasions.

In 1955, Admiral Collins was assigned to be commander of Cruiser Division One in the Pacific, responsible for the operations of three heavy cruiser divisions which covered an area of 50,000 miles—visiting Japan, Hong Kong, Singapore, and Melbourne. He became assistant deputy chief of naval operations for logistics in 1957. On a visit to London, the senior admiral in London gave a reception for him, to which I was invited, being at the time on the staff of the senior admiral. When I became the top woman officer later that year, he and Peggy gave me a very lovely luncheon.

In 1958, the president of Bethlehem Steel offered Admiral Collins an interesting job at its shipbuilding plant in Quincy, Massachusetts, where the company was building some of the surface nuclear ships for the navy. He retired from the navy and accepted the job, which necessitated his spending a great deal of time in Washington. There, we met when a mutual friend, Admiral Giles

Stedman, president of U.S. Lines, gave a reception for Giles's Washington friends. At the party, Admiral Collins told me that Peggy had died. During the next two years, we saw a great deal of each other. In December 1960, we announced our engagement at a party we gave at the Army Navy Club in Washington. I don't know how the press found out, but the *Washington Post* and the *Washington Star* both carried stories about our engagement.

We planned to be married in the Navy Chapel in Washington and then go to Europe for our honeymoon. As usual, however, there was a navy crisis, and personnel were restricted to two weeks leave, which was too short for such a trip. I went to see my boss, Vice Admiral W. R. Smedberg III, to ask him if I could have a month rather than the two weeks. He readily agreed. At our weekly staff meeting, he said to the other officers, "I have granted Winnie a month's leave for her honeymoon. I don't want any of you male officers to think that I'm giving her special privileges just because she is our only woman captain—any of you men who marry an admiral will be granted the same amount of leave."

On April 22, 1961, Rear Admiral Collins and I were married in the presence of many of our navy and civilian friends. We left for Paris via Pan American Airlines the next morning on a trip that took us to Monte Carlo, Nice, Rome, Venice, Milan, Zurich, Copenhagen, and London. At each city we met navy friends which added so much to the enjoyment of our trip.

⚓ ⚓ ⚓

Wedding picture of Captain Collins and her husband Rear Admiral Howard L. Collins, at the Navy Chapel, Washington, D.C., April 22, 1961.

In order to spend more time with my husband, I decided to retire and make my retirement date effective August 28, 1962, which coincided with my twentieth year in the navy, the earliest I could retire to receive retirement pay. I could have stayed on active duty but I would have had to revert to the rank of commander as my predecessor had done because the law specified that the navy could only have one line captain. I had served five years as captain, so it would be only fair for me to leave that assignment.

Once my decision was made, I began to say my farewells. A very special occasion for Howard and me was a joint review of the graduating class of women recruits at the Recruit Training Command at Bainbridge, Maryland. This was an historic event, as it was the first time two naval officers—husband and wife, rear admiral and captain—took a navy review together. This would be my last formal review prior to my retirement. We were honored to present to Seaman Apprentice Elaine J. Peters, graduating with this class, the American Spirit Honor Medal, the top award given to the most outstanding naval recruit. She was also chosen by her company to receive the Military Award for her company.

From July 26 to 29, 1962, the WAVES twentieth anniversary was celebrated in Washington, D.C. Some 2,000 women officers and enlisted arrived from all parts of the country. I gave a speech giving an up-to-date report on the status of navy women and the new opportunities available to them in assignments and advanced education. Mildred McAfee Horton, (the former Mildred McAfee), was the toastmistress and Admiral Claude V. Richets, vice chief of naval operations, gave the evening address. Our guest list included the secretary of the navy and many of the senior officers stationed in Washington. During our celebration, I presented to President John F. Kennedy at a White House ceremony two volumes of a first British edition entitled *History of the American Navy*, by James Cooper. In addition, I presented another book, *Bits and Pieces of American History*, containing reproductions of beautiful old prints and paintings about navy subjects, which we hoped would be a valuable addition to the White House library. President Kennedy responded very graciously and complimented the women of the navy on their achievements.

Rear Admiral Collins and Captain Collins review enlisted women's recruit graduation, June 1962. Official U.S. Navy photograph.

Commander Irene Wolensky and Captain Collins present two rare navy books to President Kennedy on the occasion of the WAVES twentieth birthday and Captain Collins's retirement. R. L. Knudsen PHC, USN, Office of the Naval Aide to the President, photographer.

A colorful art show was on display in the Statler Hotel, the convention headquarters. Included were portraits of navy women leaders, starting with Captain Mildred McAfee Horton, Captain Jean Palmer, Captain Joy Bright Hancock, Captain Louise Wilde, and a recently completed portrait of me. In addition were water-color sketches of navy women at various activities which were sponsored by the curator of the Navy Combat Art collection. My husband spoke to the convention audience. In closing, he said, "I am the only admiral in the history of the U.S. Navy who is an aide to a captain, and I love the job."

My service as assistant chief of personnel for women was in its last weeks. My boss, Admiral Smedberg, asked if I would come to his office early in August. He told me that he wanted me to have a formal retirement similar to that given an admiral.

"I think we owe you that honor," he said. "And if it weren't for the restriction of the law, you would most assuredly be an admiral."

I thanked him but protested my having such a formal retirement. He would not accept my protest and said, "Does August 9 suit your schedule? I'd like to get the invitations out and have arrangements made for both an enlisted male and female honor guard. Also, my invitation will include a reception at the officer's club and it is my pleasure to pay for it."

The ceremony took place as planned at Leutze Park in the Potomac River Naval Command in Washington. Along with a platoon of sailors, a twenty-six member enlisted woman honor guard from the Recruit Training Command was on hand. Uniform for the officers was full dress white (with medals). The enlisted and honor guards uniform was summer ceremonial. Dozens of admirals were present as was the chief of naval operations, my good friend Admiral George Anderson, and his wife Mary Lee, the secretary of the navy and two assistant secretaries, and many women officers and enlisted women. I inspected the troops and honor guard. Chief of the Chaplain's Navy Corps Monsignor George Russell delivered a beautiful invocation. I gave a short speech, the most important part of which conveyed my deep and sentimental feelings about my navy career:

> On this occasion, I feel it is appropriate that I express those special blessings which I feel are mine:
> (1) The magnificent blessing of being an American woman who has had the good fortune to serve in the United States Navy for the past twenty years.
> (2) The opportunity of knowing the many unselfish and wonderful men of the navy whose dedicated service has been such an inspiration to the navy women. By their example, we have learned the true meaning of pride of service.
> (3) The privilege of being director of the women of the navy and knowing the many thousands of fine women who made this assignment so rewarding.

The ceremony was a very moving experience for me. Present was my relief, Captain Viola Sanders, the new chief of naval personnel for women. So many memories came to my mind at this time. I was pleased with my twenty-year career in the navy and especially my past five as assistant chief of naval personnel for women. I thought of some accomplishments I was able to make as captain, although I knew there were many things that still needed to be done for women in the navy.[4] I thought too of the underlying goal of all my work: We navy women wanted to be equal professional partners with navy men. For my accomplishments over the period 1957–1962, I received two commendations: the Legion of Merit and the Secretary of the Navy's Commendation. The first is one of the highest military awards for military personnel.

My husband was at the ceremony in uniform although he had retired from the navy. He selected the music. The band serenaded me with "I'll See You Again" and then they quickly swung into, "She's Just a Sailor's Sweetheart" as we walked off the field to the

Captain Collins congratulates her successor, Captain Viola Sanders, at retirement ceremony at Leutze Park, Navy Yard, Washington, D.C. on August 9, 1962. Official U.S. Navy photograph.

officer's club for the reception. Howard's son Jack, a Naval Academy graduate and an air force lieutenant colonel flyer, flew in from California with his wife. Also present was my aunt, Margaret LaPointe Jones from Vallejo, California. The reception was wonderful with so many of my good friends present.

The press asked me what I was going to do after I retired. I said, "I'm going to give full time to my hobby—spelled with a 'U' [for Hubby]." I was later to learn, however, that "full time" still allowed me "spare time" to do some other professional work, which involved stimulating activities I thoroughly enjoyed.

---

[1] Data supplied by Naval Historical Archives, Washington Navy Yard, Washington, D.C. 20374.

[2] In my tour pregnant women, married or unmarried, were discharged from active duty with no exceptions. In 1972, this policy was modified. If a pregnant woman requested to remain on active duty, her case was reviewed and in most cases was approved. In 1982, the pregnancy policy was again modified so that a pregnant woman was not automatically released from active duty. Each case was reviewed separately. If a woman had obligated service, she was retained on active duty unless physical conditions did not permit continuance on active duty.

[3] The leader of the Soviet Union at the time.

[4] For my assessment of what needed to be done to improve the status of women in the Navy after 1962, see Chapter 8.

seven

RETIREMENT . . . SORT OF

After I retired from the navy, I received a number of tempting job offers. One was from a large investment company that offered me many favorable incentives to become a broker. But my five years as assistant chief of naval personnel for women had been a demanding and difficult assignment and I did not want to accept another full-time job. My husband, Howard, had quit his Bethlehem Steel Corporation job and we were looking forward to leisure activities and travel.

Howard was eager to have me play golf and so was I—until my first game. I had never had time for golf before but I was used to tackling difficult tasks, so I approached this first game with much confidence. It was a disaster! My husband told me I was holding the club like a baseball bat, which I am sure accounted for my weird shots. I barely survived that first game and delayed further golf exposure with him until I took some lessons, which I did not tell Howard anything about. The next time we played golf, he complimented me and said that I'd made considerable improvement. I continued my secret lessons and practice. One day I beat my husband, which absolutely astounded him. After that, he used to tell his friends that his one ambition in life was to beat me in golf. I even got to enjoy the game! When I confessed to him that I had taken golf lessons, he said that was a pretty sneaky way to beat him.

In our first leisure trip, Howard and I went to Hong Kong, Taiwan, Thailand, and Japan. We then spent the rest of the winter with many navy friends in Honolulu, which was a wonderful and relaxed time. By then, I had the courage to play golf several times a week with Howard and friends. Soon, although I was enjoying my leisurely retirement, I wanted something professional to do. But I knew I needed a professional opportunity that would still allow flexibility for leisure activities.

The first opportunity came from the president of Women's Life Insurance Company, who invited me to be a member of her company's board of directors. Formed in 1961, Women's Life was the first legal reserve capital stock life insurance company limited to insuring females. It targeted women because it could offer favorable premium rates stemming from women's greater longevity, less hazardous work, and lower suicide and disability statistics than men's. Also, the employment of a person to do the household and child-caring work of a wife who had prematurely died cost a huge amount of money. Although the firm insured all women, its primary focus was on sales to female military personnel and service wives. The work sounded challenging to me. I accepted the offer and became a director, serving as military advisor in the public relations program aimed at active and retired military personnel and dependents of military men.

This work fit in nicely with my retirement plans. It did not take too much time, since I served mostly as a consultant, and I was both professionally and intellectually interested in the work. I wrote a number of articles for the company about the importance of a professional woman or a housewife having insurance. My articles pointed out that because a husband in most cases thinks that his wife does not need insurance, he is unaware of the costs he would face in raising a family in the event that his wife dies. It was a totally new idea to most men. Unfortunately, the company failed because it was based on ideas about ten years ahead of its time. Insurance to cover the loss of a wife and mother is now an important part of family planning.

Bob Barnum, a U.S. Steel executive and a vice president of the National Navy League, presented me with the opportunity for my next professional involvement when he sent me a complimentary letter about my career and enclosed a gift membership in the Navy League for Howard and me. It was a very kind gesture, since to become a member of the Navy League a person has to be recommended by a current member. No active duty military person can be a member.

The Navy League was formed in 1902 by President Theodore Roosevelt for the purpose of educating people about the importance of sea power to protect U.S. commerce and maintain national security. It has several hundred councils in the United States and overseas, and its membership is approximately 70,000 patriotic civilians, industrialists, and retired personnel of all services, including individuals with commercial interests involving trade— such as importers and exporters—industrialists who build our ships, and ordinary citizens with concerns about naval matters.

Shortly after I became a member of the District of Columbia Navy League Council, I was elected as a director. About two years later, Bob Barnum told me that he wanted me to be chairman of the national nominating committee, whose job it was to select the president and ten vice presidents of the national organization. The election that was coming up was a critical one, as there were strong political pressures for two of the candidates. Bob and the two current vice presidents of the Navy League I met with felt that because of my reputation, my appointment as chairman would be a signal to the membership that the meetings would be conducted fairly and that the committee would select as its president a person who had high qualifications and a record of integrity. It was vital to have a president of the Navy League who would be respected by navy, marine, and Coast Guard leaders.

As chairman of the national nominating committee, I had the Navy League's judge advocate, J. Paul Marshall, sit next to me because I was fairly new to the organization. He knew the by-laws; I didn't. The committee reviewed the qualifications of the candidates and evaluated their contributions to the league. Although it was a difficult and secret session for our committee, we nominated an excellent and highly intelligent corporate lawyer from Chicago, Morgan Fitch, to be the president. We also nominated ten vice presidents and 200 directors. On one occasion when I was out of the room for a few minutes, the committee selected me as one of the ten vice presidents. The other nine they chose were men. When I came back to the room and the committee informed me of what they had just done, I said, "There is no way that I could possibly accept that. I am chairman of the nominating committee and I am not nominating myself!"

"This is a decision of the nominating committee," a committee member said. "The chairman does not have a vote. Our recommendation will have to go before the 200 members of the Navy League board of directors. They will have the final decision."

The board voted me in. I was honored to be chosen as an official of such an eminent organization, particularly since I was the first woman vice president in the Navy League's history. Like my fellow vice presidents, I received no pay for my work. I became chairman of the National Public Affairs Committee and became very active in my work. At this time, the government was making deep reductions in the defense budget, and one proposal was to cut the number of ships in the navy. I had many other tasks during these troubled times, which included getting midshipmen assigned to work with Navy League councils throughout the United States and overseas. Through speaking engagements at civic events and interviews with television, radio, and newspaper journalists, the midshipmen were to play a public relations and recruiting role for the Naval Academy and the Coast Guard Academy.

The program was highly successful. In 1972, over a three-day schedule, the Naval Academy midshipmen participated in public relations activities in nineteen states and Puerto Rico. They had 135 speaking engagements at civic and community events,

Captain Winifred Q. Collins is elected as the first woman vice president of the National Navy League. Seated from left, William J. Weinstein, Leon I. Porett, James M. Hannan, Captain Collins, Carl Neisser. Standing from left, Robert E. Bateman, Albert S. Horwath, James V. Grealish, Joseph F. Call, Jr., Peter Kirill, Thomas E. Morris. Official U.S. Navy photograph.

appeared on fifty-two radio and television programs and received press coverage in fifty newspapers. In some instances, their combined television, radio, and newspaper audiences comprised more than a million people. They brought before the public their fine appearance, poise, and speaking ability and attracted many young men to apply to the Naval and Coast Guard Academies.

I was responsible for obtaining the services of Norman Polmar, U.S. editor of *Jane's Fighting Ships*, to do a series of articles for the Navy League's *Sea Power* magazine which assessed the current state of U.S. and Soviet combat and merchant strength. Specifically, the articles listed the types of combat ships, including the numbers of destroyers, cruisers, submarines, and aircraft of both the United States and the Soviet Union, and gave the estimated combat potential of each.

I had many other interesting assignments with the National Navy League. During 1966–1967, while I was vice president and national membership chairman, membership rose from 38,000 to 41,000 and the league's distinguished group of life members increased from 718 to 835. I was asked by the Navy League's president to do a management study of their headquarters, whose organizational structure was just a mishmash. The staff needed clear-cut definitions of their duties and responsibilities that directed them toward our Navy League goals. Yet the lines of authority from each vice president down to the staff were unclear. My strategy was to organize the staff to support the programs of each vice president. I did a study of everyone's job and changed what I thought the duties of each job should be so that it would conform to our overall Navy League strategy. The president and board of directors approved the new personnel staffing program.

While I was a vice president, I was concerned about women's participation in the Navy League. I pointed out to my colleagues that there are many capable women leaders in our country—both community leaders and professional women—and I recommended that we make a special effort to increase the number of women in the league and then utilize them to stress to the public, including community leaders and educators, the importance of U.S. naval power. The president replied that he would also like more minorities in the Navy League. "I know Winnie doesn't like to be classified as a minority," he said, "but we would like more women in the league, too."

"No, Winnie doesn't like women being classified as a minority because they aren't," I said. "Actually, males are now the minority and women constitute the majority—48 percent to 52 percent."

I tried to get more women into leadership roles in the organization, but I did not have much success. I was frustrated with the lack of responsiveness by the men to attract women to the league and give them responsibility. They had the same chauvinistic ideas and prejudices that I had encountered in the navy, and I fought the same uphill battle to get them to accept the intelligence and ability of women. I finally had every past president of the Navy League supporting me—and they eventually elected another woman vice president.

During my six years as a vice president, I worked on a nuclear aircraft carrier controversy in the face of heavy opposition. I organized a public relations program with factual materials about the importance of having a sea-based carrier that could move around the oceans without refueling. The materials included speeches, press releases, editorials, feature articles, and fact sheets supporting the need by the United States for a carrier for the strategic, tactical, and political goals of our country. The packets were sent to Navy League councils with suggestions on how this material should be used in newspaper articles, speeches, and television and radio programs. My program had a very positive impact on the issue. The many letters received by the president of the Navy League from senior naval officers, congressional leaders, and prominent civilians attest to the importance this project played in assisting the navy to obtain legislative approval for the carrier.

Another one of my appointments in the Navy League was as chairman of the awards committee, which selected members who had made outstanding contributions to the goals of the Navy League. I am proud of the Navy League's accomplishments and my part in its achievements.

In 1971, Secretary of the Navy John H. Chafee awarded me the Distinguished Public Service Award for outstanding service to the United States Navy, citing my work in the field of public information and community relations when I was national vice president in the Navy League. This is the top navy award given to a civilian.

In 1973, the Navy League awarded me the Distinguished Service Award of the United States for making the most outstanding

Secretary of the Navy John W. Chafee presents Captain Collins with the Distinguished Civilian Public Service Award. May 14, 1971.

contribution as a Navy Leaguer. And in 1992 I was inducted into the Navy League Hall of Fame, which is made up of individuals who have been members of the Navy League for twenty-five years and have contributed outstanding service to its national objectives.

⚓ ⚓ ⚓

Admiral Louis Denfield, president of The Retired Officers Association (TROA) and a former chief of naval operations, asked me in 1964 if I would be a director of this organization. Like most organizations of that time, TROA had never had a woman officer on its board of directors. I had known Admiral Denfield during my navy career and was pleased to accept his offer. I remained a director for eight years.

TROA is made up of men and women officers, active and retired, who served as officers in military services of the United States. Formal directors' meetings took place only twice a year, but I spent a lot more time than that on the organization's committees. One of the responsibilities of the president of the association was to choose a chairman of the finance committee. Unfortunately, assuming that a senior military male officer was capable of handling all jobs, the president had chosen a marine colonel who actually knew nothing about finance. Because of my years of experience with my own portfolio and my graduate work in business, I later took over that job and helped build up the organization's financial resources.

One objective of the association was to assist TROA members and their wives in any of their legal problems as well as protect the benefits of military personnel. One of the goals the organization sought and achieved was to provide benefits for widows of officers, who previously were not eligible for any monetary benefits. I participated by letters and speeches in military wives' clubs on subjects of interest to military wives. Because I was instrumental in attracting retired women officers into TROA, I was pleased when later many of these women assumed leadership roles at both the local and national levels of the organization.

⚓ ⚓ ⚓

In 1972, during the Vietnam War, Admiral Elmo Zumwalt, Jr., chief of naval operations, asked me if I would be a trustee of a foundation called Helping Hand, the purpose of which was to raise funds for South Vietnamese navy families. Admiral Arleigh Burke, Anna Chennault (vice president of Flying Tigers Line), and many other prominent civilians and military officials were members. As Admiral Zumwalt told me:

> The economic problems plaguing the Vietnamese navy may be as detrimental to their cause as the enemy. With the very low salaries, the very high cost of living, and the inability of the navy or government to meet the needs of its personnel on active duty or the needs of its veterans, widows, and orphans, they are left to live in squalid living

conditions. With the humanitarian help of American sailors and the financial assistance of the Helping Hand Foundation, we can do much to improve their living conditions,
diet, and morale.

I accepted this assignment as trustee but felt that it was important for me to investigate how we were spending the millions of
dollars collected. With Admiral Zumwalt's approval, my husband
Howard and I flew to Saigon in a military aircraft (at no expense
to the taxpayers). When we arrived in Saigon about 3 A.M., a driver
was waiting for us. En route to our hotel, he drove without lights,
explaining that night hours were the most dangerous because the
enemy came out then to attack vehicles on the highway. We were
grateful for his caution and relieved to arrive safely at our hotel.

This was a fascinating trip. It was also scary, as the war was
not far away, and the sound of the rockets was close. We spent
three days in Saigon evaluating how the Helping Hand funds were
benefiting the Vietnamese navy families. One important item was
the procurement of cinder blocks, with which the Vietnamese
could build houses that were a tremendous improvement over
the shanties they were living in. Helping Hand also imported top-
grade pigs and poultry—plus feed—to augment the Vietnamese
people's diet with more protein. Because the climate was so hot,
the foundation purchased navy-style large refrigerators and freez-
ers where the pork, chickens, fish, and eggs could be stored. A
U.S. Army officer who had graduated from an agriculture program was teaching the Vietnamese how to add many lines to their
fishing boats instead of relying on only one. This procedure in-

creased the number of fish that could be caught. With this extra amount of protein, some of the Vietnamese children grew twelve inches in one year.

My aide was a charming Vietnamese navy woman lieutenant who introduced us to the children in their classrooms. They captivated both Howard and me, as they were so well mannered. With the aide's help, I tried to greet the children in their own language and tell them how attractive they were and how much it meant for us to meet them. Since there are so many different intonations in the Vietnamese language, my few words sent them into bursts of great laughter. The aide wouldn't tell me what I had actually said.

It was a heartwarming and memorable experience to meet these gracious and charming Vietnamese. Howard and I both felt that the foundation was doing a tremendous job by helping the

Cinder block housing provided by the Helping Hand Foundation. 1972.

Captain Collins and Rear Admiral Collins visiting a schoolroom in Vietnam in connection with their work for the Helping Hand Foundation. 1972.

members of the Vietnamese navy, their families, and the widows and orphans. After South Vietnam was conquered by the communist forces of North Vietnam, however, Helping Hand was dissolved.

⚓ ⚓ ⚓

In 1972, Under Secretary of the Navy Frank T. Sanders asked me to be a member of his navy educational board of advisors. In addition to me, there were fifteen other civilian members, including Bruce Davidson, academic dean of the U.S. Naval Academy, who was a highly intelligent and charming person. We worked closely for six months, until February 1973. Our assignment was to visit and review the navy's recruit training and advanced training schools for enlistees and all of the postgraduate schools for officers, then to make recommendations concerning needed changes.

At this time, by executive order, the military services were required to take a percentage of recruits of a low intellectual level who lacked basic educational skills, a policy based on the notion that the services would improve skills and provide career opportunities for these less qualified recruits. In one of our visits, we inspected the Recruit Training School at Orlando, Florida, where we discovered to our dismay that the school had eighteen male recruits who were unable to repeat the alphabet but still had been recruited. They had been held over for a second period of training because they were incapable of performing even the lowest jobs. It was our observation that the program was not only costing the military services far too much money, but it was also responsible for much frustration among the less qualified recruits, many of whom could not pass a test to get promoted to the next enlisted level and consequently could not qualify for a rating and increased pay.

We completed our survey and made our report to the secretary of the navy, recommending that the program was costing military services a tremendous amount of money to try to improve the skills of recruits who lacked the mental abilities to qualify for the skilled ratings. We recommended that the services should not have to accept these individuals, as there were few jobs for them in the military for which they would qualify. Our recommendations were implemented, and eventually this program was discontinued for the military forces.

⚓ ⚓ ⚓

In 1977, Admiral George Anderson, former chief of naval operations, called and asked if I would be interested in being a trustee of the U.S. Naval Academy Foundation, as he would like to nominate me to its board. At that time, all the trustees were men—civilians and military officers, most of whom had served in the navy or marines. All former chiefs of naval operations were trustees. I became the first naval woman officer trustee of the Naval Academy Foundation, an organization that provides financial aid for prospective appointees to the Naval Academy who meet all of the requirements but perhaps are low in one subject, like chemistry, mathematics, or physics, or need additional education in these and other subjects. Trustees fund the scholarship program for students so that they can attend prep schools for one year to bring them up to the required academic level. Without that special help, the students might fail because their academic background could not meet the high Naval Academy academic standards. This program has been a tremendous success, helping hundreds of young men and women. Since I had such a financial struggle to get through college myself, I wanted to do something for other students. My husband and I sponsored a $20,000 honor scholarship in the name of Rear Admiral Howard L. Collins and Captain Winifred Q. Collins. Our contributions added to funds given by other trustees. I have been very proud of the exceptional candidates—ten men and women—our scholarships have helped. All have subsequently been appointed to the Academy.

In 1986, I established scholarships at three universities that I had attended. These scholarship awards were $5,000 each for a woman graduate student in the School of Business at the University of Southern California (USC), Harvard Business School, and Stanford University. In 1987, I continued two scholarships for $5,000 at both USC and Stanford. In 1994, I increased the scholarships to $10,000, allowing two awards at each university. Twenty-seven women students have been awarded an MBA with the help of these scholarships.

In 1988, I established five $1,000 scholarships for women midshipmen enrolled in the NROTC program at universities across the country. Although these students receive their tuition and books at no cost to themselves, they must pay for their own living costs. Most of these women come from less affluent families, so they have to earn their living expenses. NROTC professors select the five winners based on financial need, leadership, academic performance, and extracurricular activities. Since 1988, forty-five women midshipmen have received $1,000 each from these awards.[1]

In 1973, the National Navy League established two awards in my honor—the Captain Winifred Quick Collins Awards for Leadership. One of these awards is given to a woman officer and the other to an enlisted woman. In both cases, either the navy or the marines commanding officers makes the nominations, which are then reviewed by the Navy League awards committee, chaired by one former secretary of the navy and including retired senior officers of the navy and marines.

Among the forty-seven navy and marine awardees—all of whom are outstanding—two are especially worthy of note. In 1984, Lieutenant Wendy B. Lawrence, a Naval Academy graduate, was the recipient. According to the awards committee, Lawrence won the award for her inspirational leadership

> while serving as a NATO Operation Officer of Helicopter Support Squadron Six and as Maintenance Officer of Detachment Three of that squadron. Her leadership, energy, and extensive knowledge enabled her squadron to achieve new levels of operational efficiency and readiness, exemplified by 25,000 hours of accident-free flying. While serving in the North Atlantic, she led her eighteen-man unit to transfer in heavy seas 843 tons of cargo and 395 passengers to twenty-three ships.

Lieutenant Commander Wendy Lawrence is now an astronaut—the first woman Naval Academy graduate to be so honored.

In 1990, Lieutenant Commander Alison E. Mueller, a Nurse Corps officer stationed at Oaknoll Hospital, received the award for her inspirational and heroic action following the San Francisco earthquake of October 17, 1989. On learning of the collapse of the freeway in Oakland, she mobilized a team of medical staff and rushed to the site. Disregarding her own safety, she entered spaces on the two-tiered bridge and searched for victims and remains, spending four sixteen-hour days on a bridge that was subject to collapse and aftershocks. She repeatedly entered spaces where vehicles were crushed and was the lead person in removing thirty-six bodies. Lieutenant Commander Mueller is now retired and lives with her marine officer husband and two children.

⚓ ⚓ ⚓

In 1977, someone from a New York executive personnel organization called and told me that a large international corporation was seeking a qualified woman to be a director, and asked if I knew who would be good for the position. The president of the corporation (CPC International), wanted a woman on the board who had been head of one of the military services. The job description sounded quite fascinating. "I'll have to think of somebody," I said to my husband.

"What's wrong with you? What about yourself?" he asked. "You have two masters' degrees in business and have had high-level international policy experience in the navy."

"I never even thought about me," I said.

I applied and sent them my resumé, along with three letters from individuals who were acquainted with my career. I chose Mildred McAfee Horton, Admiral George Anderson, and Ambassador Sam Berger. The ambassador was a career foreign service officer of the United States who had known me and my husband for many years.

A week later Jim McKee, president of CPC International, called and asked if I could be free to come to the corporate headquarters in Englewood, New Jersey—just outside of Manhattan—to have lunch with him and several company vice presidents and directors. I flew to New York on the appointed date. A chauffeured limousine picked me up at the airport and took me to the headquarters, a beautifully decorated building of three floors—each of which covered one acre.

CPC International is a multinational corporation located in the United States and sixty-two foreign countries, with annual sales of over $10 billion. They produce a large number of different food products including corn oil, English muffins, peanut butter, mayonnaise, soups, and many other high quality grocery products. Jim McKee, three vice presidents, and four outside directors greeted me for lunch. McKee asked me if I would like a cocktail.

"Ordinarily, at lunch I wouldn't," I said. "But with eight men to converse with, I don't think I will have much time to eat." They all laughed and ordered cocktails, too. It was a delightful luncheon. I was asked many questions about my navy life, graduate education, hobbies, and other matters.

"Would you have time to be a director?" Mr. Mckee asked.

"Yes, I would," I replied. "I enjoy being busy and can turn off activities to make room for more interesting ones."

The president then guided me through a tour of the headquarters. I enjoyed the meeting and the luncheon, but after returning to Washington I didn't hear a word from CPC for a couple of months. Jim McKee's secretary finally called in late August and said that he had been on vacation but was eager to meet with me at my home in early September. I couldn't understand why he wanted to come to my home, but I agreed.

He arrived on the appointed day and told me that the fifteen male directors of the board had enthusiastically approved my nomination to be a member of the board of directors. I was very pleased and asked him to express my appreciation to the board members, but I asked him why he hadn't just called me with the news.

"I felt that our first woman director should receive the news in person from me," he said.

Most of my male co-directors were presidents of large U.S. corporations, and I was frankly impressed with their status. At my first meeting, one of them asked me, "Are you a Women's Lib supporter?"

"I don't think I'm a Lib, and I'll tell you why," I replied. "I went into a men's restroom by mistake once and I honestly didn't think it was that fascinating."

He laughed and said, "I think you're going to be a challenge."

"I hope I will be," I replied.

I was appointed to the board of directors in September 1977. Part of my duties would be traveling with my husband to CPC's plants throughout the world and meeting with the plant managers. Luckily, the company's policy had always been to encourage spouses to travel, too. Howard and I decided to go to Asia in January 1978 for our first visit to CPC's plants. We went first to Hong Kong, headquarters for the company's operations in Asia. The president for CPC Asia was Paul Craven, an outstanding executive who briefed us regarding the company's operations in eleven countries representing 940 million people with a gross national income of $806 billion. Our schedule for this trip also included visits to Thailand, Malaysia, Singapore, the Philippines, and Japan. Each visit included a briefing by the plant manager and his staff with information on profitability and items produced. We inspected the manufacturing process, and we received political and personnel management information. Each plant had a top Swiss chef who produced the soups, peanut butter, and mayonnaise to suit local tastes. Our trip was a whirlwind adventure. I felt the travel experience was a very important indoctrination for me.

Howard and I were very much impressed with CPC's management and top personnel. After each day's visit, we were entertained by the staff, employees, and wives. As a female director of such a large corporation, I was somewhat of a novelty to the many international personnel and especially to the wives. We completed the Asian visit in two weeks, and I was to give my report at the upcoming board meeting. Before the meeting, two of the directors with whom I had become friendly asked me what I had been doing. I said that Howard and I had been to Asia to visit CPC plants in six Asian cities: Hong Kong, Bangkok, Kuala Lampur, Singapore, Manila, and Tokyo.

"Well, we've never been invited to go on a trip overseas. The president suggested that you make the trip because you are a woman."

If anything is a red flag to me, it's the suggestion that I've gotten some special privilege because of my gender. I thought at first they were kidding me, but I finally decided that they were serious, and I knew I had to say something about it.

After I finished my report to the board, Jim McKee asked, "Did you encounter anything that had a negative impact?"

"Yes, I did. I ran into the worst case of reverse discrimination I have ever encountered."

"What in the world was that?"

"Jim, why won't you let the male directors travel?"

All the directors stood up and roared in laughter.

"Winnie," the president said. "I told the male directors the same thing I told you. But for their benefit I'll get out a written directive that authorizes overseas travel for them." And so the other directors started to travel overseas. When they returned from their trips, they said, "I had a nice trip and it's all thanks to you, Winnie."

The board met once a month. I was assigned to the pension fund investment committee involving millions in funds. After one of our meetings, the president asked me if I would like to be chairman of a committee. I replied that I would love it, but when I told Howard about it, I also said: "This is a very tough assignment because they are currently losing three percent in the investment funds. I hope I can handle it." My committee consisted of five corporate presidents, and I was concerned that they would be more knowledgeable than I was. Howard tried to reassure me that they wouldn't begin to have my investment knowledge, and he was right. After two years, when I turned the chairmanship over to Howard McGraw, the president of McGraw-Hill, our investment strategy was successful and we were earning a high return in the pension fund.

Each director is periodically rotated from one committee to another. After I left the pension committee, I was assigned to the executive committee, which controlled salaries and assignments for top executives in the United States and CPC International posts around the world. Other committee assignments followed. All in all, my work at CPC was a very stimulating experience. I had one of the best times of my life at the corporation. I retired in 1984 after seven years as director. My successor was a brilliant U.S. career ambassador, Jean Wilkowsky, who lives in Washington, D.C. She became one of my best friends.

⚓ ⚓ ⚓

If retirement from the navy allowed me more time to spend with my husband, it also gave me time to keep in touch with my family in a way I had not been able to do before. I had seen my mother only occasionally after leaving her in Lewiston, Idaho. In 1935, she and my brother Larry lived with my sister Evelyn in Los Angeles for a short period. When I graduated from college in 1935 and was married, I would see them occasionally. I used to send my sister $25 a month out of my $125 salary to help take care of the expenses of my mother and Larry. Later, my mother remarried, and she continued to live in Los Angeles. Her husband was not an intellectual like my father—but it was my mother's life, not mine.

When I was in the navy, I saw her from time to time and continued to assist her financially. Moreover, I would always bring her some nice gift, such as a dress or coat. Fortunately, I never revealed to her how badly she had hurt me when I was thirteen and she left town without telling me. In later years, my mother's husband had a pension from the army and they had social security coming in. Still, they didn't have enough money to live on. My brother Dan, my sister Evelyn, and I supplemented their income. After her husband died, my mother continued to live in Los Angeles in a nursing home, and we helped support her until she died in 1966 at the age of eighty-six.

Because my younger brother Larry was in the navy, I had managed to maintain better contact with him. When I was captain, he was also in Washington, D.C., assigned to the Bureau of Naval Personnel. We saw a lot of each other then. He married and he and his wife had three children. He stayed in the navy longer than I did, retiring as a captain in Honolulu in 1975 after thirty years. He then became a real estate agent in Honolulu and he continues to work there in that business.

My brother Dan married before World War II. He returned quite ill with malaria from his army service in New Guinea. I remained close to him and his wife, who died of cancer in 1963, a terrible emotional blow for him. Later, he went to Alaska where he managed a chain of theatres. The malaria continued to bother him. His health further declined. I thought that the Veterans Administration (VA) could help him through one of their hospitals, but they turned him down.

When I was a director of The Retired Officers Association, I met some VA officials, including the number two officer. I went to see him and told him about Dan's malaria, and said I did not understand why the VA had turned my brother down. The next thing I knew I had a glowing letter from Dan, who wrote: "I don't know what happened. But the VA called me and accepted me as a patient and has given me a private room. I'm writing letters for some of the GIs, which pleases me so much that I can be useful."

Dan was in a VA rehabilitation program for seven years in Seattle and left of his own volition. He moved into his own home and was well on the way to recovery. One night while he was asleep, a faulty electric wire burst out in flames. When the flames reached the blanket that covered him, it erupted because of the flammability of the material. He made it to the kitchen door and then collapsed and died from the smoke inhalation. I called my brother Larry, who flew out to Seattle from Hawaii. Howard and I went out there, too. We arranged for Dan's funeral, burying him in an army cemetery.

My sister Evelyn's marriage with her first husband ended in divorce, but that did not bother me. I despised him because of the way he treated me when I was so young and lived with them. After she left him, she moved to Los Angeles. We were in the midst of the Great Depression. Jobs were scarce, but she was able to find one. I introduced her to a close friend of mine who was a co-owner of a drug store right on the campus of USC. Their relationship blossomed into love and they later married. They moved to Santa Barbara where he had two financially successful drug stores.

I had always been close to Evelyn because she gave me the affection I needed. But she began drinking, and she and her husband separated. She was given one of the drug stores. One day in 1953 when I was working in San Francisco, a doctor called me and told me how her condition had deteriorated because of her drinking problem. He said, "Some member of the family must come down and do something about her." Larry said he couldn't come, so the problem was mine.

I went to Santa Barbara and appeared before the judge to have her committed to a psychiatric hospital for rehabilitation. I was practically in tears, as I loved her very much. I was able to get her committed, but in three days, she just charmed her way out of there. Her problem of drinking continued, so I used to go to Santa Barbara every weekend and try to help her manage her drug store. I damaged my own health from the stress of taking on this responsibility in addition to my own busy navy assignment. Evelyn ultimately lost her store because of her inability to manage it. Later, she developed cancer and died in 1972.

My great joy during my retirement was that I was able to devote so much time to my husband. We had a magnificent marriage, traveling a good deal and leading a delightful life. The good times were marred by a health problem he developed. One side of his heart was beating ten times faster than the other side, and by the time this condition was discovered, his lung was damaged. He lost weight and his health went steadily downhill. When his doctor told me in 1979 that my husband had one year to live, I never let Howard learn that news. I gave him wonderful and loving care. I kept him on a high protein nutritious diet and looked after him constantly. That year and every year afterward, we went out to Coronado, California, for three months. In 1983, when we came back to Washington, he had gained thirty pounds. His doctor said, "Winnie, I don't believe in miracles but you certainly have produced this one."

The year went by, and Howard was better. And then one day in 1984, when we were in San Francisco for a CPC meeting, he caught a virus.[2] We flew back to Washington and Howard entered

Bethesda Naval Hospital. The doctors could not reverse the lung condition and he died on June 3, 1984. He had lived with his health problem for five years—not one year, as the doctor had predicted. I was devastated. I had two miserable years trying to adjust to my loss, and I guess I will never fully recover. But I am grateful for those extra years with him, and treasure each of the twenty-three years of our marriage.

---

[1] In 1972, Secretary of the Navy John H. Chafee authorized females to be enrolled in the NROTC program.

[2] I would travel to CPC for directors' meetings every month.

eight

NAVY WOMEN: YESTERDAY, TODAY, AND TOMORROW

O n the fiftieth anniversary of the founding of the WAVES—
July 30, 1992—2,000 Navy women who had been officers
and enlisted personnel assembled in Norfolk to celebrate five decades of service to their country. On hand were some of the
nation's leading military and political figures carrying messages
of appreciation for the contributions that navy women had made
to national security over the years. Some of the women present
that day had joined the navy with the first group of WAVES volunteers, just like I had done. They were now in their eighties and
nineties. But navy women from every decade since the 1940s were
also there, and women who were currently on active navy duty—
most of whom were in their twenties and thirties—were on hand,
too. The assembling of 2,000 navy women for this occasion sym-
bolized a common bond of fellowship uniting generations.

For me, the day was one of nostalgia. I renewed old friendships with women who had been members of my class at Smith
College as well as other navy women I had worked with throughout my twenty years of military service. I was thrilled to meet with
the intelligent, purposeful, and professional young women who
were on active duty. I shared with them memories of my navy
days, but I also learned from them about the thoughts and aspira-
tions of today's navy women.

Our navy women's anniversaries are times for joyous celebration, but they are also occasions for reflection. They are markers
by which we measure how far we've come and signals by which
we think anew about how far we have yet to go. A fiftieth anniversary is a time for even more reflection than most others because it covers such a long time span in any person's life. Both in
my speech at Norfolk as well as in my thoughts, I evaluated the
changes in the status of navy women. In World War II, women
signed up in the navy as volunteers, committing themselves to
service because of the shortage of manpower. They had no idea
that the navy would ever offer a career for women since, like other
services of the military establishment, the navy was a male preserve.

Women in World War II performed their military duties with
distinction. They worked under severe restrictions. At first, they
could only serve in the continental United States; the scope and
responsibility of their assignments were limited; and a glass ceiling prevented them from rising beyond the rank of commander.
The extraordinary requirements of World War II helped open up
new opportunities for navy women in jobs usually held by males,

allowing them to move into technical fields which had been re-garded as the exclusive domain of men. Then, women were per-mitted to serve in Hawaii, and in 1945 one woman was even assigned to Alaska.

When the war ended, most of the navy women—like the male reservists—went home. During demobilization, the navy found it necessary to retain some female reservists, and a directive was sent out requesting volunteers to remain on active duty. Some 400 women officers and 1,600 enlisted women volunteered. In the late 1940s, however, the requirements of world politics made the permanent participation of women in the armed services a necessity. The Cold War between the United States and the Soviet Union meant that we would have a continuing need to be pre-pared for war. A changing military technology, which reduced the significance of distance as a protector of U.S. national security, indicated to navy leaders that there had to be a nucleus of women on active duty so that navy women could quickly be mobilized during periods of national military crisis. In 1948, women became part of the regular armed services.

Although the law recognized the importance of women to the armed forces, it still imposed severe restrictions on them. More-over, women—especially enlisted women—experienced a consid-erable amount of resistance from their fellow male servicemen, many of whom saw them as obstacles or competitors to their own professional development. Nevertheless, because of navy women's professional distinction, the support of some key political and navy leaders, and the constant fear of war, the barriers against navy women slowly began to break down. Navy women themselves were the prime movers in their own advancement. Those who had preceded me as either director of the WAVES or assistant chief of naval personnel for women paved the way in supplying leadership. I particularly want to pay tribute to the work of these pioneers: Mildred McAfee, Jean Palmer, Joy Hancock, and Louise Wilde. But women at all navy ranks—from officer to enlisted, from commander to seaman—played equally important roles improving the life of navy women and, of course, the efficiency of the navy itself.

I was proud to make my own contributions, helping women receive new and challenging assignments, attend advanced schools which gave them new educational opportunities, and have access to leadership incentives. I was able to gradually remove many of the restrictive policy regulations that had blocked their careers. As captain, I made every effort to have women officers and enlistees detailed by the male assignment officer, helping to place women in new kinds of jobs as well as integrating them into the overall assignment program of the navy.

⚓ ⚓ ⚓

I knew when I retired in 1962 that the next generation of navy women would succeed in removing even more of the barriers. And they have done a terrific job in doing just that. In the 1970s, the navy had moved to an all-volunteer force. Since many men were not interested in a military career at this time, there were shortages in manpower. Consequently, women seized upon the chance to join the navy and to take on jobs that had been held only by men. In 1972, Captain Alene Duerk, director of the U.S. Navy Nurse Corps, was selected as a rear admiral, the first woman unrestricted line officer to achieve flag rank.

In 1973, the secretary of the navy authorized aviation pilot training for women. In 1978, the law was changed to permit women to fill sea billets on support (supply) and noncombatant ships, and a policy in compliance with the law was immediately initiated. Navy women became pilots and other members of the flight crew, although they were still forbidden to operate in either combat aircraft or combat ships. Women were admitted to the Naval Academy for the first time in 1976, and the first women Academy students graduated with the class of 1980.

In 1997, we have 7,941 navy women officers on active duty representing thirty-five percent of total officer strength. Of this group, 541 are assigned to combat airwings and ships. There are 244 captains, four rear admirals (lower half), one rear admiral (upper half), one rear admiral (lower half selectee), and one vice admiral.[1] There are 45,900 women enlisted on active duty representing 12.5 percent of total enlisted strength. In combat airwings and ships, 3,621 enlisted women are presently assigned.

Navy recruitment efforts have been successful in recruiting African Americans and other minority men and women. In December 1945, the navy had two African-American women officers and seventy enlistees. In 1948, when women entered the regular navy, there were no African-American women officers and only six enlisted women. By the third quarter of 1993 (the last time these statistics were available), the navy had 691 African-

American women officers and 13,028 enlisted women on active duty.

Many practices for women that existed in the navy for years have been swept away as the navy comes to terms with personnel management. For example, in 1972, if a pregnant woman—married or not—requested to stay on duty, the navy normally gave approval. In 1975, a pregnant navy woman was not automatically permitted to stay on active duty, even though she so requested. Each case was reviewed individually. In 1988, a pregnant woman would not automatically be released from active duty even though she had so requested. If she had obligated duty, her request was denied unless other circumstances indicated it was in the best interest of the navy to release her.

Shortly after I retired, I received a call from Admiral Jimmy Holloway III, chief of naval operations. "You'll be so pleased with what I've done," he said.

"What have you done?" I asked.

"I've designed a uniform for active duty women who are pregnant."

"Oh, no," I said. "Just let them wear civilian clothes. Otherwise, every mother in America will think that all women in the navy are pregnant."

He was very disappointed with my reaction to his pregnancy uniform.

"Ask your wife about my opinion on this subject," I said. And she agreed completely with me, of course. Now, however, there is a pregnancy uniform not only for navy women but for women in all the military services.

The navy has also designed for navy women a white summer work uniform, shirt, skirt, and trousers (optional) similar to the male uniforms. I think it's most attractive.

⚓ ⚓ ⚓

There has been much opposition within the military as well as in our society against women in combat. I told our 2,000 women at the 1992 convention that I really felt navy women were overtrained for it: "We have been in combat for fifty years." I received a cheering response from my audience.

From a practical point of view, navy women have already served in combat, as their experience in the Persian Gulf War attests. When they were on the ships that were resupplying the aircraft carriers and battle groups in the Persian Gulf and the Red Sea, they were certainly at risk—along with their male contemporaries—of becoming combat casualties. The Gulf War showed how difficult it is to separate women from combat not only in the navy but in all services. According to the Women's Research and Education Institute, more than 33,300 U.S. military women served in key combat-support positions in Operation Desert Shield/Desert Storm. They served as pilots and crew members in planes and helicopters, directed artillery, drove trucks, ran prisoner-of-war facilities, served on support, repair, and hospital ships and in port security units and construction battalions, and performed many other military functions in this war zone. The lifting of the combat restriction is a timely recognition of military women's intelligence and ability.

⚓ ⚓ ⚓

The women who enroll today in the navy are responsible and well-educated citizens. They are going to the top navy and civilian schools and are taking on newer and more challenging assignments with each passing year. In my opinion, service in the U.S. Navy has become one of the finest professions a woman can follow, with many opportunities for new jobs, travel, promotion, and retirement greater than those in the civilian sector. Navy women officers can even be admirals. With combat duty now authorized, eventually, one of them may even hold a senior assignment in the navy, or become president of the United States.

There are still navy men who think that having a woman as top navy "man" would be unthinkable. But as this book shows, navy women have made tremendous progress. In 1942, I could not imagine women admirals holding key navy assignments.

Whenever I think about the negative comments men make about the talents of navy women, my thoughts inevitably return to the days of my early childhood. I remember that when I was a little girl, my father taught me that there are no insurmountable barriers to what women could accomplish. "I hope to Heaven I live long enough to see a woman president because the men have made such a mess of things," he said.

He didn't live long enough to see a woman president, nor have I—so far, at least. But his words and hopes for women are an inspiration to women not only in the navy but in all other walks of life in the United States as well as to women throughout the world.

---

[1] A rear admiral lower half has one broad single stripe. A rear admiral upper half has one broad stripe plus one single narrow stripe. A vice admiral has two single narrow stripes above the broad stripe.

appendix

BIOGRAPHICAL INFORMATION

Year of birth: 1911, Great Falls, Montana

Education:

University of Southern California, B.S., 1931–1935

Radcliffe College (Harvard–Radcliffe Graduate Program in
Administration), Certificate, 1937–1938

Stanford University, M.A., 1951–1952

Navy Service:

Commissioned Ensign, U.S. Naval Reserve, August 1942

Personnel Director, U.S. Naval Reserve (Smith College and
Mount Holyoke), September 1942–1943

Member, Navy Department Management Team, 1943

Planning Officer, Bureau of Naval Personnel, 1944

Director of Naval Personnel (Women), Commandant's Staff,
Hawaii, for assignment of 5,000 WAVES, 1944–1946

Planning for transfer of women to Regular Navy and establishment of promotion and rotation policies, 1946–1950

Commissioned Lieutenant Commander, U.S. Regular Navy,
1948

Secretary of Defense Staff, 1950–1951

Stanford University, 1951–1952

Director of Personnel, Commandant's Staff, San Francisco,
1952–1956

Staff of the Commander in Chief Naval Forces, Eastern Atlantic
and Mediterranean at London, Management, 1956–1957

Chief of Naval Personnel for Women, 1957–1962

Retired from the Navy, 1962

Citations:

Military:

Legion of Merit

Bronze Star Medal

Secretary of the Navy Commendation Medal

American Campaign Medal

World War II Victory Medal

Asiatic Pacific Medal

National Defense Medal

Civilian:

1971 — Navy's Distinguished Civilian Public Service Award

1973 — Distinguished Service Award of the Navy League

1990 — Inducted into the National Navy League Hall of Fame

1994 — Nominated to the International Hall of Fame of
Professional and Business Women

Married: Rear Admiral Howard Lyman Collins (U.S. Naval Academy
graduate)

Post–Navy Experience
National Vice President and Director of the United States Navy
League, 1965–1985
National Director and Chairman, National Navy League Awards
Committee, 1984–present
National Director, The Retired Officers Association, 1964–1972
Director, Women's Life Insurance Company, 1964–1966
Consultant to the Department of Health, Education, and
Welfare, 1966, 1967
Trustee, Helping Hand Foundation for Vietnamese navy
families, 1972
Member, Secretary of the Navy's Board of Advisors on Education, 1976
Vice President of the Republican Women's Club of the District
of Columbia, 1976–1977
Director, Harvard Graduate Business School Club of Washington, D.C., 1980
First woman Director, CPC International, Inc., 1977–1984
Trustee, United States Naval Academy Foundation, 1977–
present

Other Data

Who's Who of American Women, Who's Who in Society, Who's Who in Finance and Industry, Who's Who in Professional and Executive Women, Who's Who of International Intellectuals
Member of International Intellectuals; Member, Two Thousand Notable American Women; Member of International Biographical Center, England; Member of International Media Association; Life Member of U.S. Naval Institute; Life Member of the U.S. Naval War College Foundation; Life Member of the U.S. National Navy League; Life Member, The Retired Officers Association

INDEX